THEOLOGICAL INTERPRETATION OF SCRIPTURE

Cascade Companions

The Christian theological tradition provides an embarrassment of riches: from Scripture to modern scholarship, we are blessed with a vast and complex theological inheritance. And yet this feast of traditional riches is too frequently inaccessible to the general reader.

The Cascade Companions series addresses the challenge by publishing books that combine academic rigor with broad appeal and readability. They aim to introduce nonspecialist readers to that vital storehouse of authors, documents, themes, histories, arguments, and movements that comprise this heritage with brief yet compelling volumes.

TITLES IN THIS SERIES:

Reading Augustine by Jason Byassee

Conflict, Community, and Honor by John H. Elliott

An Introduction to the Desert Fathers by Jason Byassee

Reading Paul by Michael J. Gorman

Theology and Culture by D. Stephen Long

Creationism and the Conflict over Evolution by Tatha Wiley

Justpeace Ethics by Jarem T. Sawatsky

Reading Bonhoeffer by Geffrey B. Kelly

FORTHCOMING TITLES:

Christianity and Politics in America by C. C. Pecknold

iPod, YouTube, Wii Play by D. Brent Laytham

Philippians in Context by Joseph H. Hellerman

Reading Revelation Responsibly by Michael J. Gorman

Theological Interpretation of
SCRIPTURE

STEPHEN E. FOWL

CASCADE *Books* · Eugene, Oregon

THEOLOGICAL INTERPRETATION OF SCRIPTURE

Cascade Companions

Cascade Books
A Division of Wipf and Stock Publishers
199 W. 8th Ave., Suite 3
Eugene, OR 97401

www.wipfandstock.com

ISBN 13: 978-1-55635-241-6

Cataloging-in-Publication data:

Fowl, Stephen E.

    Theological Interpretation of Scripture / Stephen E. Fowl.

    xvi + 92 p. ; 20 cm. — Includes bibliographical references.

    Cascade Companions

    ISBN 13: 978-1-55635-241-6

    1. Bible—Hermeneutics. 2. Bible—Criticism, interpretation, etc. 3. Bible—Theology. I. Title. II. Series.

BS476 .F68 2009

Manufactured in the U.S.A.

Contents

Acknowledgements

When this project was first proposed to me, I was not eager to accept it. I felt, and still feel, that I am too close to many of the crucial debates, issues and people involved in theological interpretation to give the type of balanced overview that one imagines with a volume of this nature. But Jim Tedrick and Jon Stock have been my friends for many years and I could not say no to them. Fortunately for all of us, they had just hired as an editor a very able young scholar named Chris Spinks. Chris already knew the issues and debates around theological interpretation very well. His help in the various stages of this project has been invaluable. He is not responsible for the errors and shortcomings in this volume, but he should get a great deal of credit for its strengths.

For longer than I care to remember, Rob Wall and I have been talking about theological interpretation. He has a passion for these issues and debates that combines a scholar's rigor, a teacher's concern for his students' learning and a pastor's ardor for the gospel and the life of the church. Although he is not a Jesuit, he is a superb example of *cura personalis*, that care for the whole person that exemplifies Jesuit education at its best. I am particularly grateful for his comments on this volume. I have not always been able to work his insights into the text, but I have always learned from them. It is my great pleasure to dedicate this volume to him.

Introduction: What Sort of a Companion Is This?

This is a companion to the Theological Interpretation of Scripture. The majority of this small volume will be devoted to its subject matter, interpreting Scripture theologically. Nevertheless, it might be useful here at the outset to reflect on what sort of companion this book tries to be. In many ways, the time is ripe for such a companion.

First, although Christians have been interpreting Scripture with an aim of deepening their life with God and each other from the very beginning of the church, the past twenty years or so have witnessed an explosion of scholarly writing devoted to the theological interpretation of Scripture. In addition, there are now a variety of institutional structures concerned to support "theological interpretation of Scripture" however that is understood. There are two sections of the Society of Biblical Literature directly devoted to theological interpretation.[1] Their sessions are almost always very well attended. In 2005 Baker Academic published a *Dictionary for Theological Interpretation of the Bible*. The *Journal of Theological Interpretation* began in 2007. Both Brazos and Eerdmans are publishing commentary series devoted to theological inter-

1. The SBL sections are Theological Hermeneutics of Christian Scripture, and Christian Theology and the Bible.

pretation of specific biblical books.[2] Thus, one of the tasks of this companion will be to explore some of the connections between this long-running and essential Christian practice and this more recent body of scholarly literature. The other central task of this companion is to help people navigate their way through the contemporary literature.

These two tasks seem basic to any companion to the theological interpretation of Scripture. Moreover, these two tasks become more interesting and perhaps complicated by the fact that the person writing this companion has been an active participant in and contributor to this burgeoning literature. Thus, I write this companion as one who has advocated particular positions in the current debates. I am a companion or at least a conversation partner of many of the parties involved in the current debates. In writing this volume, I also propose to be your companion, introducing you to people, texts, and issues that have become quite important to me over the years.

It is as if I have invited you to accompany me to a large and somewhat chaotic party. I will try to help you join the party by introducing you to friends, acquaintances, and some with whom I respectfully disagree. I am certain that my choices will shape the way you experience the party. Some ideas, thinkers, and arguments are, to my view, superior company to others. Nevertheless, I will introduce you to others as best and as truthfully as I can. My hope is first, that you will join the party and participate in your own right, and second, that you will not come to feel that you were brought in under false pretenses.

2. Brazos Theological Commentary on the Bible and The Two Horizons New Testament Commentary.

There are four parts to this companion. The first part looks at discussions of Scripture, its nature and role in God's drama of salvation. This is relatively brief. It is, nevertheless, important to the account of theological interpretation for which I advocate here. If one has a grasp of what God's ultimate desires for us are and how Scripture fits into God's plans ultimately to bring those desires to fruition, then theological interpretation of Scripture will need to be closely tied both to our proper end in God, that is, God's ultimate desires for us, and Scripture's role in bringing us to that end.

One aim of the second part of this companion is to survey a variety of concerns that are often connected to or seen as central components of theological interpretation. The first of these is the dominant concern of professional biblical critics with matters of history and that collection of diverse (and often incompatible) interpretive strategies called "historical criticism." It will be important to examine briefly some of the issues that arise when historical matters are seen as primary to theological concerns with regard to theological interpretation. Further, the most common and significant way in which the concerns of historical critics seek to influence theological interpretation is through the discipline of biblical theology. Although the manner of theological interpretation advocated here will find work in these fields useful on an *ad hoc* basis, I will try to explain why these matters are ultimately less crucial to theological interpretation than many others think.

In addition to historical concerns, there are very significant approaches to theological interpretation that place great weight on matters of philosophical hermeneutics. There is a great deal to be learned from these approaches. Ultimately, however, I want to indicate that there is a significant theological price to pay by giving hermeneutical concerns priority over theological and ecclesiological concerns.

This will lead to the third part of this companion in which I will try to explore those practices and habits and concerns that are crucial to theological interpretation. I will argue that matters of ecclesiology, confession, forgiveness and reconciliation, truth telling and admonition, and friendship and conversation are central to theological interpretation of Scripture. In short, I will argue for the priority of theology and ecclesiology to philosophical or general hermeneutics.

A brief fourth section will lay out several prospects and issues for future consideration. This is potentially the most idiosyncratic part of the companion. That is, based on my own understanding of the central issues and debates among those engaged in theological interpretation of Scripture, I will venture to suggest some future directions for theological interpretation and some debates that may need to take place.

The final section is the one I am most cautious about. There I will try to speak clearly and charitably about central figures in current debates over theological interpretation. Although I have learned from all of these figures, I also have some substantial disagreements with some of them. My aim here is more to try to situate their work than to criticize it, though inevitably some of that will happen. In addition, I will, no doubt, leave out some important scholars whose work should be engaged by students interested in theological interpretation. This final section can in no way substitute for a student's serious and direct engagement with these scholars' works. In addition, I do not include my own work in this discussion. Everything I say in the first four parts of this companion is a way of situating my own position relative to others. Although I do not consider my views set in stone, I can at least narrate briefly how I came to hold the views I do.

Early in my graduate studies I became very frustrated with what I took to be the hermeneutically unsophisticated and theologically arid state of biblical studies. I and many others my age found great encouragement in the writings of Brevard Childs and Anthony Thiselton. These two scholars in particular made it seem possible to combine serious philosophical and theological concerns with critical sophisticated study of the Bible. Indeed, I found that most of the American PhD programs in which I was interested would not easily accommodate these interests. As a result, when I got the opportunity to study in Sheffield with Anthony Thiselton, it was an easy choice to make.

The Department of Biblical Studies in Sheffield was a wonderfully vibrant place in the mid-1980s. In addition to a very generous faculty, my fellow graduate students, including Mark Brett and Gerald West, were enormously influential in helping me think through a variety of issues. My research on Paul's hymnic language and speech-act theory helped me to bring a variety of theoretical concerns to bear on some christologically important texts in the New Testament. As I completed that project it appeared to me that although it had been a good form of therapy for my views about language, speech-act theory would be of only limited use in interpreting texts. Further, it seemed to me that the real significance of combining hermeneutics and biblical studies would appear in matters around the use of Scripture in ethics.

This led me to the work of Alasdair MacIntyre, and then to Stanley Hauerwas, and finally to my erstwhile colleague, L. Gregory Jones. As Greg and I finished *Reading in*

Communion I realized that my focus on ethics as an outworking of an interest in hermeneutics and Scripture was too narrowly conceived. Christian ethics is inseparable from theology. Unfortunately, contemporary biblical studies and theology were two disciplines often devoted to keeping each other at arm's length. I expected that philosophical hermeneutics would be the bridge between these two. I also knew that this chasm had not always been there. Hence, I began to read more and more pre-modern biblical interpretation in hopes of finding ways of spanning the chasm between biblical studies and theology.

A sabbatical year in Dublin thinking and talking with Lewis Ayres about pre-modern biblical interpretation helped teach me that rather than applying the Bible to theology, at its best, Christian interpretation of Scripture was a type of theology. This led me to see that both attempts to organize the theology in or of the Bible in terms of biblical theology and systematic concerns with philosophical hermeneutics were not going to be as useful for interpreting Scripture theologically. Instead, it would be important to understand the ends and purposes of the Christian life and Scripture's role in achieving those ends. In addition, ecclesiology and specific ecclesially based practices would provide better resources for interpreting Scripture theologically. *Engaging Scripture* is my attempt to begin to address these concerns.

When I was invited to contribute a volume in the Two Horizons Commentary Series, I was eager to try a comprehensive piece of theological interpretation rather than simply to talk about how to do it. The discipline of commentary writing is a wonderful opportunity to figure out what theological interpretation might look like in practice. *Philippians*, however, is but one way of doing this and should not be taken to rule out other options.

This, of course, is a far more coherent account of things than I ever could have offered when I was in the midst of each episode. No doubt further work may also lead me to revise this story. Yet this is how I see things now.

At this point I should also note that shortly after beginning this project I was sent the manuscript of a very fine introduction to the theological interpretation of Scripture by Dan Treier.[3] It is a judicious account of many central issues in theological interpretation. As he says in his introduction, the aim of this book is "to tell the story" of the current interest in theological interpretation and to "map the major themes of this movement" (11). He also wishes "to address some tough questions and to clarify this movement's future direction" (11). Treier's is an introduction in the best sense of that term. He provides students with a reliable and appropriately critical map of the terrain. So, how, aside from the obvious differences in length, is this "companion" different from Treier's "introduction"? As a way of concluding this introduction let me offer some answers to this question. I hope, however, that it will become clear that students of theological interpretation will want to engage both Treier's "introduction" and this "companion."

As I said above, I am an interested party in matters of theological interpretation. As a Christian scholar, I am compelled to treat all views charitably. I will not pretend, however, that mine is a neutral account of issues regarding theological interpretation. Treier's book, while not claiming neutrality, is

3. Treier, *Introducing Theological Interpretation of Scripture.*

closer to that ideal. If Treier seeks to introduce students to theological interpretation by providing them with a map, this companion aims to help students navigate a specific course through the conceptual issues and scholarly writing surrounding theological interpretation. Thus, I hope to present theological interpretation of Scripture in a way that will help form students to read Scripture with a certain set of aims and interests.

With this agenda in mind, let us begin by looking at Scripture, and how discussions about Scripture's nature and purpose can decisively shape how we view the theological interpretation of Scripture.

ONE

Scripture: Its Nature and Place
in God's Drama of Salvation

It seems like a good idea to begin a companion devoted
to the theological interpretation of Scripture by thinking
theologically about Scripture. This is because how and what
Christians think *about* Scripture will influence the ways in
which Christians might interpret Scripture theologically.
Of course, it is not always clear how to separate theological
thinking *about* Scripture from theological interpretation *of*
Scripture, since much theological thinking about Scripture is
closely connected to Christian views of God, the world, and
God's relations with the world that are themselves drawn in
various ways from Scripture.

As Origen's *On First Principles* and Augustine's *On
Christian Teaching* indicate, these issues were traditionally
treated together. It is not my aim to separate what belongs
together conceptually and theologically. Rather, I am simply
treating these as two distinct topics for the sake of organiza-
tional clarity.

Initially, then, I want to begin by thinking about Scripture
in theological terms. Most modern attempts to address the
place and status of Scripture begin by asking what sort of

1

book Scripture is.[1] On the one hand, modern historical studies have made it all too clear that Scripture is a human work. The original texts that comprise the Bible were written by a variety of human authors (known and unknown) in diverse historical, linguistic, and cultural settings. Both the human authors of these texts and those who preserved, edited, and ordered these texts participated in and were subject to a host of social, material, and institutional forces which undoubtedly affected the composition of the Bible, even if scholars are not altogether sure how and to what extent this happened.

At the same time, Christians are committed to the notion that Scripture is the word of God. In, through, or in spite of its clearly human, historical characteristics, Christians confess that Scripture repeats, conveys, or reflects the words of the living God. At the very least, this makes Scripture the standard against which Christian faith and practice need to measure up.

If one begins by focusing on Scripture's status as both the word of God and the work of human hands, it seems quite natural to extend a christological analogy to Scripture in order to account for its status as both divine and human writing. That is, in ways that are analogous to the confession that Christ has two natures, human and divine, Scripture is taken to be both human and divine. Although there are some premodern theologians who deploy a christological analogy to account for various ways in which Scripture might function, the use of a christological analogy to account for Scripture's status seems to be quite modern.[2] Moreover, although this analogy is fairly common across theological and denomi-

1. See for example Work, *Living and Active*, 1–14.

2. Ayres and Fowl, "(Mis)Reading the Face of God."

national differences, it is less clear that theologians use this christological analogy in the same way.

For example, Karl Barth applies a christological analogy as a way of taking Scripture's "writtenness" seriously: "there is no point in ignoring the writtenness of Holy Writ for the sake of its holiness, its humanity for the sake of its divinity."[3] Taking Scripture's writtenness seriously in Barth's eyes seems to allow for some types of historical exegetical methods, though Barth is appropriately wary of the exhaustive claims of historical criticism.[4] Because Barth fundamentally orders his views about Scripture in the light of his doctrine of God, treating Scripture's writtenness seriously means primarily treating Scripture as the hermeneutical lens through which one views all other things.[5] As a result, Barth's use of the christological analogy does not demand any specific interpretive practices.

From the Roman Catholic side of things, Vatican II's Dogmatic Constitution on Divine Revelation (*Dei Verbum*) also relies on a christological analogy in its reflection on Scripture. In this case, the analogy works to show that human language can be a suitable vehicle for conveying God's word. "God's words, expressed through human language,

3. Barth, *The Doctrine of the Word of God*, 463. See also Work, *Living and Active*, 68–74.

4. Barth, *The Doctrine of the Word of God*, 469. Barth seems to avoid theologically corrosive historical-critical claims by stressing Scripture's role as human witness to a divine "subject matter." Barth takes this subject matter as self-evident. Subsequent Marxist or feminist biblical critics, however, simply extend the suspicion that the historical critics of Barth's day applied to the text of Scripture to the Bible's "subject matter." This renders claims about the self-evidence of the text's subject matter quite problematic.

5. Ibid., 468.

have taken on the likeness of human speech, just as the Word of the eternal Father, when he assumed the flesh of human weakness, took on the likeness of human beings."[6] Because this is a claim about God's willingness and ability to work through human language, the claim neither demands nor recommends any particular form of interpretation.

In contrast to both Barth and *Dei Verbum*, it has recently become much more common for this christological analogy to be applied to Scripture in the way advocated by Ernst Käsemann and many others. For Käsemann, this application of a christological metaphysic to Scripture results in or justifies a further set of interpretive arguments and practices.[7] First, Scripture's human historical status necessitates the wide variety of practices commonly known as historical criticism. Failure to see this, Käsemann argues, is to lapse into a sort of docetism. Failure to employ historical criticism is an implicit denial that Scripture is really the work of human hands. Because the Bible is a human book, it should be subject to the same interpretive practices and standards as any other ancient text. In this light, the interpretive practices and theories of biblical scholars should be accessible to all regardless of one's disposition to the claims of Judaism or Christianity. Should an interpreter be a Jew or a Christian, those convictions need to be abstracted as much as possible from one's interpretive work as a biblical scholar. Biblical interpretation becomes an end in itself whose goal is either the unearthing or the construction of textual meaning(s).[8]

6. *Dei Verbum* §13 in Tanner, *Decrees*, 2:977.

7. See Käsemann, "Vom theologischen Recht historisch-kritischer Exegese."

8. Adam has noted the ways in which Käsemann's argument fails

Upon deciding to treat the Bible as a human historical text to be read like any other, the remaining issue for theologians and Christians more generally is how to treat the Bible as the word of God. Once interpreting the Bible as a human book becomes its own end, the question is how to move from the results of that work either to theological claims, or to the moral and ascetical formation of Christians, or to any other edifying practice which Christians have traditionally based upon Scripture.

One older approach to this problem of how to treat the Bible as the word of God after already treating it as the work of human hands attempted to distill the timeless truths of Scripture from the historical particularities of the biblical texts and those texts' production. The so-called "biblical theology movement" represents the most recent form of this attempt.[9]

Such attempts rarely stand the tests of time. It is usually just a matter of a few years before any given proposal about a unique or timeless scriptural theme is shown to have some sort of cultural or temporal antecedent. When scholars adopted the christological analogy as a justification for reading the Bible as any other book, it became evident that critical scholarly activity would seek to fit the texts of the Bible into their historical and cultural milieu without remainder. This

---

(see Adam, "Docetism, Käsemann, and Christology"). The Pontifical Biblical Commission's report *Interpretation of the Bible in the Church* is the Catholic version of this way of thinking about the dual natures of Scripture. Recently, Brent Strawn has argued that although Adam's argument may work well against historical criticism, it may not fit Käsemann himself (see Strawn, "Docetism, Käsemann and Christology").

9. Brett, *Biblical Criticism*, 76–115.

leaves little of theological interest or usefulness on which to build. The failures of theological approaches to Scripture that primarily operate on this christological analogy suggest that one should try an alternative starting point.

In his recent work, *Holy Scripture: A Dogmatic Sketch*, John Webster points out that doctrines about Scripture must begin with and depend upon doctrines about the triune God.[10] The Christian God is the Trinity, whose inner life is reflected in the gracious and peaceful self-giving and self-communication of Father, Son, and Spirit. In creating all things, the triune God does not simply freely will the existence of humans created in the image of God, but God also desires fellowship with humans, offering them a share in the divine life. This is both the intention with which God created and the end for which God created. Given this, God's self-presentation or self-communication is an essential element in establishing and maintaining the fellowship God freely desires to have with humans. Thus, God's self-revelation to humans is both the source and content of a Christian doctrine of revelation. Revelation is directly dependent upon God's triune being and it is inseparable from God's freely willed desire for loving communion with humans.[11] In this light, the written text of Scripture is subsidiary to and dependent upon a notion of revelation that is itself directly dependent on God's triune being.[12]

This recognition recalibrates the relationships between God, Scripture, and Christians in several interesting ways. For Christians, the ends of reading, interpreting, and embodying

10. Webster, *Holy Scripture*, 5–41.

11. Ibid., 13–15.

12. See *Dei Verbum* §2.

Scripture are determined decisively by the ends of God's self-revelation, which are directed towards drawing humans into ever-deeper communion with the triune God and each other. In this way, scriptural interpretation is not an end in itself for Christians. One might even say that Scripture itself indicates that the mediation of revelation through written Scripture is not God's best desire for believers but a contingent response to human sinfulness. Recall that God speaks with Adam and Eve with an unbroken immediacy. This is also reflected in the description of God's interactions with Moses as speaking with a friend face to face (Exod 33:11). Further, Jer 31:31–34 indicates that the written covenant will ultimately be replaced by a covenant written on the heart so that teaching, remembering, and interpreting Scripture will be a thing of the past. In addition, when confronted with Moses's permission of divorce in Deut 24:1–4, Jesus makes it quite clear that there is a gap between God's best intentions for humans and the scriptural words of Moses which are offered as a concession to human sinfulness (Matt 19:1–9). These texts indicate that Scripture is the result of God's condescension to human sinfulness. At the same time, Scripture is absolutely important since it reveals the mystery of God's reconciling of all things in Christ. Thus, although the interpretation and embodiment of Scripture is not an end in itself, as Christians engage Scripture "for teaching, for reproof, for correction, and for training in righteousness," they can confidently advance toward their proper ends in God, "proficient [and] equipped for every good work" (2 Tim 3:16–17). Until God's law is written on our hearts after the manner of Jeremiah 31, Scripture is a sufficient means for revealing the triune God to sinful humans.

Another avenue that opens up when Christians think of Scripture in the light of their convictions about the triune God is in relation to the history and processes of the formation of Scripture. An emphasis on Scripture's dual nature will obviously recognize that the text of Scripture as we know it today is tied to a variety of historical, political, and social processes. Scholars may disagree about the nature of these processes, but it is hard to deny that a variety of forces, known and not known, shaped and were shaped by the text of Scripture.

This recognition becomes difficult to square with a doctrine of revelation if that doctrine is divorced from its subsidiary role in relation to the doctrine of God. As Webster argues, just such a divorce occurred in the history of modern theology. Rather than a doctrinal assertion related to God's triune identity, theologians came to think of revelation as an epistemological category requiring philosophical rather than theological justification. "Understood in this dogmatically minimalistic way, language about revelation became a way of talking, not about the life-giving and loving presence of the God and Father of our Lord Jesus Christ in the Spirit's power among the worshipping and witnessing assembly, but instead of an arcane process of causality whereby persons acquire knowledge through opaque, non-natural operations."[13] Once one moves in this direction it becomes easier to understand why some attempts to defend the divine nature of Scripture tend to focus their attention on establishing either the incorruptibility of the text or the benign nature of the processes by which the texts of Scripture come to us. The most extreme manifestation of this concern is found in those theories or

13. Webster, *Holy Scripture*, 12.

doctrines of Scripture that require some form of divine dictation where the human authors of Scripture simply record the words the Spirit speaks to them.

Even though scholars probably know much less about the processes that shaped the final form of Scripture than we are willing to admit, it is indubitable that every stage of this process was fully historical and fully human. Thus, if this epistemologically focused doctrine of revelation persists, it really becomes impossible for the christological analogy of Scripture's dual nature to hold. It would seem that at this particular point the divine and human natures of Scripture simply cannot co-exist. "Both naturalism and supernaturalism are trapped . . . in a competitive understanding of the transcendent and the historical."[14]

Alternatively, if revelation is seen as the triune God's self-communication, an activity that flows from the very nature of the Trinity, an activity that is graciously directed to drawing humanity into ever deeper communion with God and each other, then one can be more relaxed in approaching and analyzing the human processes that led to the formation of Christian Scripture. This is because the triune God is not simply the content of revelation, but the one who directs and sustains the revelation of God's very self with the aim of drawing humanity into ever deeper communion. The conviction that God's revelation is ultimately directed towards bringing about our salvation also entails a view of God's providential ordering of history so that God's ends ultimately will be achieved. In this way, Christians can fully recognize the human processes (whatever they may have been) that led

14. Ibid., 21.

to the formation of Scripture. At the same time, their convictions about God's providence should lead Christians to understand that, however Scripture came to look the way it does, Scripture reveals all that believers need to sustain a life of growing communion with God and each other.

In this respect, Christians would do well to take on the disposition displayed by Paul in Phil 1:12–18. In this passage the imprisoned Paul begins by noting that, contrary to what one might expect, the gospel has advanced even in the midst of his imprisonment (v. 12). Indeed, Paul's adoption of the passive voice here makes it clear that God, and not Paul, is the agent advancing the gospel. Paul then goes on to note that many believers in Rome (most likely) have become bold in proclaiming the gospel. Paul further observes that among these newly emboldened preachers, some preach from good motives and others preach from selfish motives (v. 15). After commenting on each of these groups (vv. 16–17), Paul surprisingly goes on to announce that, no matter what the motives of these preachers, Christ is being proclaimed, and Paul rejoices in this (v. 18).

The motives of the preachers, while important, seem secondary to the act of proclamation. It may appear that Paul pragmatically prefers to see the gospel preached than to wait until everybody's motives are pure. I do not think Paul sees the choice in quite this way. Ultimately, Paul is convinced that God is directing both his personal circumstances and the more general spread of the gospel. Thus, he need not be overly concerned about the motives of any particular set of preachers. Paul is able to see in the midst of his own circumstances that, despite appearances and contrary to expectations, God is advancing the gospel. Rather than expressing a preference for preaching from selfish motives over no preaching at all, this phrase is an expression of faith in God's providential oversight of the gospel's progress.

From a theological perspective it is important to note that a very particular doctrine of providence underwrites Paul's account here. Paul is confident that God will bring the good work started in his own and the Philippians' lives to its proper completion (1:6). Paul's view of God's providence leads him to fit himself and his various circumstances into a larger ongoing story of God's unfolding economy of salvation. Within this larger context, and only within this context, Paul's circumstances can be seen as advancing the gospel. This view of providence enables Paul to rejoice even in the face of a gospel proclaimed from selfish motives. This is because the advance of the gospel is subject to the larger ends of God's economy of salvation. If this disposition is extended to Scripture, Christians can both recognize the vicissitudes in the historical formation of Scripture and still treat Scripture as God's providentially ordered self-revelation.

Obviously, one cannot sustain any notion of God's providence apart from a fairly robust notion of the Spirit's role in the various aspects of Scripture's formation. One's initial thinking about this should start from the role Jesus anticipates for the Spirit in the lives of those who will come to produce Scripture as presented in John's Gospel. The Spirit is the one who calls to mind all that Jesus taught (John 14:6). Jesus also promises that the Spirit will lead his followers into all truth, truth that they simply could not bear on that side of the crucifixion and resurrection (John 16:2–15). In addition, the Spirit will guide and direct the disciples concerning what is to come so that they can continue to abide in Christ (John

15:1–11). In remembering the past words of Christ, leading and confirming the disciples in all truth, and speaking about the things yet to come, the Spirit's role in the lives of believers, and thus in the production of Scripture, is comprehensive.

The Spirit's work in the operation of God's providential ordering of things sanctifies the means and processes that lead to the production of Scripture, turning them to God's holy purposes without diminishing their human, historical character. Thus, in calling Scripture "holy," Christians are not making a comprehensive claim about the purity of the motives of the writers and editors of Scripture. These may well have been decidedly unholy. Even in the face of such unholy motives and actions, Christians are committed to the belief that the triune God has revealed a passionate desire to have fellowship with them, even in the light of their manifest sin. Scripture is chief among God's providentially ordered gifts directed to bringing about reconciliation and fellowship with God despite human sin. Thus, Scripture is holy because of its divinely willed role in making believers holy.

QUESTIONS

1. What does it mean to think of Scripture as both a divine and a human document?

2. Why is it important to connect a view of revelation to God's identity as Trinity?

3. Why is a robust notion of God's providence important for understanding Scripture?

TWO

Theological Interpretation
and Its Relation to Various Other Concerns

In the first chapter, I offered an account of Scripture and its place in the life of God and its role in the ongoing drama of our salvation. Scripture needs to be understood in the light of a doctrine of revelation that itself flows from Christian convictions about God's triune life. Scripture is a gift from the triune God that both reflects and fits into God's desire to bring us into ever deeper fellowship with God and each other.

This claim has presumed what I take to be the relatively uncontroversial assertion that the end or *telos* of the Christian life is ever deeper communion with God and each other. Although various Christian groups may characterize this in terms of "friendship with God" (Aquinas), *theosis* (Orthodoxy), glorifying God and enjoying God forever (Westminster Confession), or simply using the word "salvation," Christians can all recognize that, at the least, "ever deeper communion with God and neighbor" suitably characterizes God's purposes for humanity.

If these convictions govern Christian thinking about Scripture and the Christian life, then Christians will come to see that they are called to interpret, debate, pray over, and embody Scripture as a way of advancing toward their true end of ever deeper fellowship with God and each other. To use images that St. Augustine first employed in *On Christian Teaching*, Scripture is the vehicle that God provides for us to travel to our true home along the road established by the life, death, and resurrection of Jesus.

Thus, in the light of such an account of the end of the Christian life, and in the light of this account of Scripture and its place in God's ongoing drama of salvation, we can begin to offer an account of theological interpretation of Scripture. That is, theological interpretation of Scripture will involve those habits, dispositions, and practices that Christians bring to their varied engagements with Scripture so they can interpret, debate, and embody Scripture in ways that will enhance their journey toward their proper end in God.

Framing theological interpretation in this way means that certain common interpretive debates such as the role of history, or authors and readers, or theories of textual meaning, will look different. In addition, other interpretive practices such as figural reading and the history of interpretation will take on new importance.[1] Further, matters that might not initially appear to be relevant to interpretation such as ecclesiology and holiness will now appear to be crucial to theological interpretation understood in this way.

There remains, no doubt, much to be unpacked in this account. I plan to do this unpacking in the next part. In this part my primary aim is to engage concerns that are often taken to be central to theological interpretation. Although these matters may be significant in themselves and may offer insights to theological interpreters, I want to indicate that

1. See O'Keefe and Reno, *Sanctified Vision*.

they will not substantially advance the practice of theological interpretation.[2]

HISTORY AND HISTORICAL CRITICISM

Open up virtually any biblical commentary written before the 16th century; then look at the discussion of that same passage in virtually any commentary written after 1870. The differences are so significant that a beginning student may well wonder if these two commentaries are actually speaking about the same biblical text. I can think of no better way to begin to think about the role of history and historical criticism in theological interpretation than to perform this exercise.

Pre-modern interpretation is very different from the types of interpretation you encounter in a modern biblical commentary or article. Understanding the nature of this difference is what is most important for now. If you have already been exposed to some pre-modern interpreters, they may seem less strange. For many students, however, their encounter with pre-modern interpretation can seem like traveling to a different planet. It may be tempting to think that the difference between pre-modern interpreters and us is that they had a naïvely literalistic understanding of the Scripture, that they read the Gospels with harmonizing eyes such that they neglected or glossed over textual puzzles. Although there may be some examples of these interpretive flaws, they are not characteristic of pre-modern interpretation at its best. Pre-modern interpreters understood that Scripture was ex-

2. The following discussion follows what I've said elsewhere in "Theological and Ideological Strategies." I am grateful to Hendrickson Publishers for permission to reproduce some of that material here.

traordinarily diverse, and contained various textual puzzles and obscurities.

For the most part, the various interpretive practices common in the pre-modern period arise from Christian theological convictions. Scripture was seen as God's gift to the church. Scripture was the central, but not the only, vehicle by which Christians were able to live and worship faithfully before the triune God. It is also the case that faithful living, thinking, and worshipping shaped the ways in which Christians interpreted Scripture. At their best, the diversity and richness of the patterns of reading Scripture in the pre-modern period are governed and directed by Scripture's role in shaping and being shaped by Christian worship and practice. Ultimately, scriptural interpretation, worship, and Christian faith and life were all ordered and directed towards helping Christians achieve their proper end in God.

It is important to understand that the difference between modern and pre-modern biblical interpretation is not due to the fact that we are smart and sophisticated while they were ignorant and naïve. Instead, modern biblical study is most clearly distinguished from pre-modern interpretation because of the priority granted to historical concerns over theological ones. Ultimately, if Christians are to interpret Scripture theologically, the first step will involve granting priority to theological concerns. This, however, is to anticipate my conclusion.

To begin then, we need to explore, at least briefly, why relatively well-known textual puzzles, ruptures, and obscurities began—sometime in the mid to late 18th century—to generate concerns that led to the rise of historical-critical methods of interpretation. In brief, during this period there was a fundamental shift in the practices of biblical interpretation. Prior to this shift Scripture was believed to be the most important of God's providential gifts for ordering, understanding, and making the world accessible to humans. In this light, Scripture presented a unified narrative through which people could develop unified, coherent views of the world. The evident diversity and rich detail of Scripture called forth a variety of reading practices, both literal and figural, that presented a common narrative. The rich variety of reading strategies characteristic of pre-modern biblical interpretation was essential if the Bible was to provide Christians with a way of rightly understanding and living within their past, present, and future.

> Since the world truly rendered by combining biblical narratives into one was indeed the one and only real world, it must in principle embrace the experience of any present age and reader. Not only was it possible for him, it was also his duty to fit himself into that world in which he was in any case a member, and he too did so in part by figural interpretation and in part of course by his mode of life. He was to see his disposition, his actions and passions, the shape of his own life as well as that of his era's events as figures of that storied world.[3]

To put the matter oversimply, interpretation here moves from text to world. This view presumes that it was often difficult to figure out how to live and move in the world in ways that would enhance one's prospects of living and worshipping faithfully before God. Scripture, despite its evident obscurities, provided a relatively clear and God-given set of lenses

3. Frei, *The Eclipse of Biblical Narrative*, 3.

for viewing the world and faithfully negotiating one's path through it.

The nature of biblical interpretation shifts decisively when the relationship between text and world is reversed in the modern period. When the world becomes seen as, more or less, immediately intelligible to all rational people, the "real" world becomes detached from its biblical rendering. In the light of this transformation,

> [t]he real events of history constitute an autonomous temporal framework of their own under God's providential design. Instead of rendering them accessible, the narratives, heretofore indispensable as means of access to the events, now simply verify them, thus affirming their autonomy and the fact that they are in principle accessible through any kind of description that can manage to be accurate either predictively or after the event. It simply happens that, again under God's providence, it is the Bible that contains the accurate descriptions.[4]

The causes of this transformation are numerous and complex. They are for the most part related to the scientific, political, economic, and philosophical upheavals that accompany the rise of what we have come to call modernity. For our purposes it is less important to explain how this transformation took place than to explain some of its consequences for the study of the Bible and theological interpretation. For example, in the light of this shift "the real" or "the historical" becomes its own realm, accessible to all, if not immediately evident to all. It is not surprising that once "the real" or "the

4. Ibid., 4–5.

historical" became its own autonomous realm, then a great deal of effort would also be devoted to developing procedures and methods for understanding and interpreting reality. This move separated scriptural, theological, and ecclesial concerns from the concerns of historical investigation. In the light of such a separation, scholars came to see historical investigation of Scripture as a discrete form of inquiry. Eventually, historical investigation actively sought to exclude theological and ecclesial concerns. Instead, scholars began to devote a great deal of intellectual effort to inquiring into the historical accuracy of the Bible.

Once the shift was made from reading Scripture so as to understand and live within the world (past, present, and future) more faithfully to reading Scripture to see if it matched up to an already known and understood reality, a gap opened up between the real world and its past, on the one hand, and the world depicted in Scripture, on the other hand. It was within this historical context, and within this set of concerns, that "historical criticism" developed.

Although people often speak of historical criticism as if it is a single organized whole, it really reflects three recurring and interrelated issues. The first issue concerns the policing of the scholar's confessional stance. Once "the historical" is presumed to be an autonomous realm it is a small step from presuming that realm is providentially ordered (whether by the Christian God or the Deist's god) to presuming that history itself must provide its own standards of meaning and intelligibility independent of one's confessional stance. Once this step is taken historical critics must seek to root out any seepage from their own or another scholar's confessional commitments into their historical work. This forced the vast majority of biblical scholars to learn how to separate their historical research from their private confessional commitments in order to participate fully in scholarly discussions.

The second issue concerns questions of the historical reliability of the biblical texts. Initially, this issue addressed the nature and scope of evidence about Jesus. Scholars focused on the character of the evangelists and their honesty. Very soon, however, the focus of this question shifted to the Gospel texts themselves as scholars tried to develop a variety of methods for getting behind their final form to find data about what really happened. Further, as more extrabiblical sources became available, they too became part of the mix of possible pieces of evidence. Rather than being a set of lenses for interpreting the world theologically, the biblical texts became relatively discrete pieces of evidence for a variety of historical questions ranging from concerns with the authors of these texts and the sources they used to the insight these texts might provide into particular periods in the history of Israel and the church.

The third issue is more complex and concerns the interpretive schema used to organize historical evidence. Once history is thought to be an autonomous notion with its own set of methods for establishing intelligibility or meaning, then scholars must not only figure out which pieces of information will count as evidence, but they will need to develop ways of ordering and interpreting the evidence.

As long as biblical scholars treated the world, past and present, as more or less immediately accessible to them, then the practices, methods, and results of historical criticism confidently dominated academic biblical study. Theological concerns were largely pushed to the margins. To the extent theological concerns received a hearing among biblical scholars it was only as those concerns arose from the assumptions common to historical critics. For Christians, this resulted in the academic subdiscipline of biblical theology. Such work often generated interesting interpretations, but did not directly contribute to the interests and ends of theological interpretation of Scripture. In short, this is because biblical theology was systematically committed to granting historical concerns priority over theological ones. Interestingly, although many Jews fully participated in historical-critical study of the Bible, they seem to have recognized the severe theological limitations of biblical theology and did not participate in it. There will be more on biblical theology below.

Scientific, cultural, political, and philosophical movements created conditions for the rise of historical criticism. The past century has witnessed great changes in the intellectual, social, and political climate. These changes worked both to undermine the dominance of historical criticism and to open possibilities for theological and ideological strategies of interpretation.

Recall that historical concerns took precedence over theological concerns in the 18th century only when people assumed they could comprehend the world and its past in more or less immediate ways, apart from the lenses provided by Scripture read theologically. Numerous genocidal conflicts, the rise of quantum physics, the ideological critiques of Marx, the psychoanalytical explorations of Freud, and many other factors now make it clear that we never perceive or comprehend the world and its past without some set of lenses.

Let me be clear at this point. The recognition that we all view the world and its past through a set of lenses and not immediately does not mean that all lenses result in 20/20 vision or that all lenses are equal. For my purposes it is sufficient to note that if the dominance of historical criticism depended on the assumption that the world and its past were immediately available to us, then the recognition that the world is not immediately available must also affect the claims of historical criticism. As a result, in the past thirty-five years, professional biblical scholarship has seen an explosion of interpretive strategies driven by scholars with particular sets of interests and commitments that go beyond presenting the past as it actually was. The most prominent of these are feminist and Marxist/liberationist strategies for interpreting the Bible.

As a result the field of biblical studies today appears much different, and more fragmented, than it did even fifty years ago. The concerns and practices characteristic of historical criticism are still around. They exist in a chastened form, however. Historical critics can no longer claim to offer us an immediate view into the past. Rather, they pursue their specific historical investigations as one among many sets of scholarly interpretive interests. The demise of the conceptual apparatus that allowed for the dominance of historical-critical interpretation of the Bible has not led to the elimination of historical criticism, nor should it. It has, however, opened the door to critical approaches to the Bible that do not grant those particular historical concerns priority over all others. This means in theory that there is now room for theological concerns to re-enter the scholarly realm. This has been slow to happen for a variety of reasons.

First, theological interpretation of Scripture never really stopped. Although it was largely exiled from academic biblical studies, Christians have been interpreting Scripture theologically because their identity as Christians compels them to do so. Reading Scripture theologically is first and foremost a practice of the church. It does not depend on the support of academics for its survival. Nevertheless, disciplined, scholarly attention to interpreting Scripture theologically can only benefit the practice within the church. Second, numerous generations of scholars came of age when historical criticism was the dominant form of academic biblical studies. Thus, the interpretive practices and strategies that arise when theological concerns and aims are given priority in scriptural interpretation fell into desuetude. Moreover, the academic practice of theology was separated from the practice of academic biblical studies. These two disciplines came to jealously guard their autonomy, making it difficult for scholars to try to work in both fields. It has only been in the past two decades that scholars have started to bridge the gap between theology and biblical studies with the aim of reinvigorating the practice of theological interpretation.

If there is to be a revival of theological interpretation of Scripture among scholars and students, we must relearn how to grant theological concerns priority over other concerns. I recognize that this is a somewhat open-ended aim. This openness is because it will not always be clear how and in what ways the priority of theological concerns will need to take shape in specific times and places. Theological interpretation will always to some degree be constituted by ongoing arguments and debates about how to bring theological concerns to bear on scriptural interpretation. At the very least, however, granting theological concerns priority will involve a return to the practice of using Scripture as a way of ordering and comprehending the world rather than using the world as a way of comprehending Scripture. Although this was the standard practice prior to the 18th century, we today will have to re-learn this habit for our own time. Before exploring this in more detail, I want to discuss other concerns that impinge on theological interpretation. In particular, I want to now take up the discussion of biblical theology, which I started above.

BIBLICAL THEOLOGY

One might simply argue that theological interpretation of Scripture primarily consists in deriving doctrines from the text of Scripture. This would be quite unsatisfying as both biblical scholars and theologians would readily agree that Scripture contains very few doctrines, especially in the form of straightforward propositions about God, humans, and the world. The overwhelming majority of Scripture is presented as narrative and poetry. One might be able to infer or derive doctrinal assertions from such texts, but those assertions rarely lie directly on the surface of biblical material. Once one recognizes this, however, the problem is not that there are too few doctrines to attend to. Instead, there are too many and they seem too diverse. Cataloging and organizing such diversity has largely been the preoccupation of biblical theology. Although one can learn a great deal from reading a good biblical theology, it is also important to understand that biblical theology is a practice that is fundamentally different from theological interpretation. Without going into excessive detail, I will try to explain here why this is so.

Biblical or even just New Testament theology covers a fairly wide range of material. My aim here is to speak of what I take to be the dominant way of doing biblical theology generally and NT theology in particular. Students should not presume that by reading this account they no longer need to attend to such engaging recent works as Wright's *The Mission of God*, L. D. Hurst's completion of G. B. Caird's *New Testament Theology*, or recent Continental works.[5] Rather, I want to identify a set of characteristics typical of the dominant strain of doing NT theology. In doing this, I hope to show the theological limitations of such work and to indicate some of the ways in which such work differs from theological interpretation as described below.

There are several good discussions of the historical development of the discipline of biblical theology. The works of Ben Ollenburger and A. K. M. Adam are particularly useful in this regard.[6] Rather than rehearse that history here, I will simply note that biblical theology generally (and NT theology in particular) manifests two persistent concerns. First, biblical theologies offer historical reports on the theological views of ancient Israel or the first Christians. Secondly, the disciplinary integrity of biblical or New Testament theology seems to depend on keeping theological concerns at a distance. Typically, biblical theologies seek to distinguish themselves from a history of religions report on the religion of the first Christians, on the one hand, and "dogmatics," on the other hand. In this light, one of the primary criticisms of NT theologies is that they step over the boundary into systematic theology.

Indeed, the discipline often seems inordinately concerned with boundaries and separations designed to keep

5. For a review of recent Continental NT theologies, see Rowe, "New Testament Theologies."

6. See Ollenburger, "Biblical Theology"; and Adam, *Making Sense of New Testament Theology*.

constructive theological concerns at bay until the NT theologian can do some more properly historical work. In this light James Barr is correct to note that "'Biblical theology' is essentially a *contrastive* notion."[7] Of course, the case is simply more extreme with Old Testament theology because of the added concern to maintain the "discrete voice" of the OT apart from the NT.[8]

This picture needs some further qualification, however. Although it seems to be important to establish biblical theology as a separate discipline, in practice many biblical theologians have never really been comfortable making their work simply a report on the religion of the Israelites or the first Christians. Such work is theologically unsatisfying. To their credit, most New Testament theologies are not satisfied with simply accounting for the diverse theological perspectives represented in the NT.

Nevertheless, one of the results of what is taken to be a thoroughly historical approach to NT theology is the recognition that the NT presents diverse theological views. NT theologies, therefore, manifest their theological concerns by negotiating issues of the unity and diversity of the NT.

In this regard there is a rather predictable pattern among biblical theologies. A biblical theologian will posit that one or

7. Barr, *The Concept of Biblical Theology*, 5. See also Adolf Schlatter's comment, "The history of the discipline of New Testament theology then confirms this in that the variations which mark its new epochs are always occasioned by outside influences," ("The Theology of the New Testament and Dogmatics," 123).

8. The emphasis on the OT's "discrete voice" comes from Child's "Toward Recovering Theological Exegesis." I discuss the theological and conceptual problems with this way of thinking in *Engaging Scripture*, 25–28.

another theological view is the controlling concept, framework, or matrix that shapes or holds together all others. Such a claim tends to generate several sorts of responses. One is to argue that the controlling concept is not "biblical," meaning that it is a theological or philosophical construct imposed on the text from outside. Given the desire to keep systematic theological concerns at arm's length, this criticism, if persuasive, is usually enough to undermine a proposal. Another tendency is simply to argue that some other perspective or concept provides the lenses that best unify the theological perspectives found in the NT.

Of course, asserting that any single concept, perspective, or theme works to unify the NT often leads others to claim that to give one perspective priority over the others establishes a canon within the canon, thus failing to treat the entire NT with equal seriousness. In the light of this charge, it is not unusual for some to claim that there is really no way to unify the differing theological perspectives in the NT, much less the entire Bible, without doing a disservice to some of these other perspectives. In response to this, NT theologians tend to move back towards a practice of simply cataloging the diverse theologies of Scripture. As noted above, this is not very satisfying theologically. This dissatisfaction then tends to start the whole process over again.

There are two important things to note regarding these typical responses of NT theologians to issues of the NT's unity and diversity. First, the recognition of Scripture's diversity is not a particularly modern phenomenon. As early as the second century, or as soon as it makes sense to speak of a stable body of scriptural texts, Christians and their opponents recognized the great diversity of perspectives within Scripture.

Indeed, to read a text like Irenaeus's *Against Heresies* it would appear that a common recognition of the extraordinary diversity of Scripture is the point from which Irenaeus and his foes both begin, even if they move in different directions.

More importantly, by separating biblical theology from other theological enterprises, biblical theologians have cut themselves off from the very theological and philosophical resources they need to manage the diversity of Scripture. The presumption of NT theologies is that the NT itself must provide whatever unity there may be amidst the diversity of the NT. Of course, if it is the NT itself which displays the diversity that is the problem, it is not likely that the NT itself will provide the solution to this problem.

Again, I think the situation of Irenaeus can be instructive for addressing this situation. Both Irenaeus and his foes began from the diversity of Scripture. Their strategies for managing the diversity, however, are quite different. As Irenaeus sees it, the Valentinians, for example, order Scripture's diversity by imposing on it a philosophical cosmology. While this provides a sort of order to Scripture it does so at some cost. First, it commits one to adopting a set of views that require so much revision of essential Christian claims about God and the world that the result is not recognizably Christian.

Secondly, Irenaeus argues that such an account is scriptural only to the extent that it is stocked with biblical verses. The result of ordering these verses within a framework provided by a Valentinian cosmology is a twisted version of the biblical story. Irenaeus likens this procedure to someone who constructed a story from Homeric verse. It is possible to take some texts from the Odyssey—in no particular order—and intersperse them with texts from the Iliad—again, in no particular order—and thus create a story. This story would contain only Homeric language; it would contain only Homeric characters. Moreover, it could easily convince the uneducated that it was a true Homeric story. Nevertheless, its connections to Homer would be only superficial and its assertions and narrative would not be Homeric at all (*Against Heresies* 1.9.4).[9]

Irenaeus's brilliant alternative is the so-called Rule of Faith.[10] Irenaeus develops an account of God's economy of salvation, which has its definitive and climactic moment in the incarnation, death, and resurrection of the Word. By clarifying the economy of salvation in the light of a crucified and risen Lord, Irenaeus can give a coherent account of the various movements of God's economy. This summary account of the whole of God's economy is what he calls the apostolic faith, a faith that is formally represented in the creed. This then provides the framework within which the diversity of Scripture can be rightly ordered so that it can be directed towards advancing the apostolic faith in the life, teaching, and worship of the church—a life, teaching, and worship that is acknowledged throughout the world (1.10.1–3). Of course, what is so striking about Irenaeus's account of the divine

9. In 1.8.1 Irenaeus uses the image of mixing up the stones in a mosaic to come up with an alternative picture. Further, as Paul Blowers notes, "Herein the struggle with the Gnostics is not just a battle of straightforward or atomized doctrinal propositions, which presumably Irenaeus could have tendered in the debate. It is more fundamentally a contention of 'our story versus theirs,' a collision of metanarratives, one Christian and one (or more) not" ("The *Regula Fidei* and the Narrative Character of Early Christian Faith," 211).

10. For a good contemporary reflection on the Rule of Faith see Wall, "Reading the Bible from within our Traditions."

economy and the Rule of Faith is that it is so clearly derived from Scripture.

Without question, there is a circular movement here. The diversity of the New Testament poses a problem that is solved by ordering that diversity in the light of the apostolic faith. Only in the light of the New Testament, however, does that apostolic faith receive its definitive formulations. As Rowan Greer puts it:

> We could say that the quest which Irenaeus accomplishes is basically the discovery of a principle of interpretation in the apostolic Rule of faith. At the same time . . . it is in another sense Scripture itself that supplies the categories in which the principle is expressed. Text and interpretation are like twin brothers; one can scarcely tell the one from the other.[11]

Of course, this circularity is not vicious as long as one recognizes that theological considerations and church tradition are intimately and complexly connected to Christian interpretation of Scripture. For biblical theology to recognize the importance of these connections, however, would ultimately undermine its reason for existing as a separate discipline.

Whether or not biblical theology continues as a coherent discipline is not my primary concern. Rather, I hope I have provided enough here to show that theological interpretation of Scripture may find the work of biblical theologians useful from time to time, but that theological interpretation is something fundamentally different from biblical theology

11. Greer, "The Christian Bible and Its Interpretation," 157.

as currently practiced. This fundamental difference lies in the fact that concerns that I take to be central to theological interpretation (i.e., doctrinal and ecclesiological concerns) are the very things biblical theology seeks to keep at arm's length, or further.

READING THE OLD TESTAMENT AS CHRISTIAN SCRIPTURE

On one level, a discussion of reading the OT as Christian Scripture promises all the excitement of a discussion of water as a liquid. Several factors, however, work to make this topic much more complicated and therefore more engaging for a discussion of theological interpretation than it might first appear. For example, there are at least two other communities of interpreters who also devote themselves to interpreting these texts from situations and with ends and purposes very different from those of Christians. These two communities are Jews and academic OT/Hebrew Bible scholars. I realize that each of these communities is really comprised of several smaller communities, and that there is some overlap in membership between some of them. For the moment, however, I would like to treat them as distinct but complex communities of interpreters. Christian interpreters of Scripture can and should engage with these two interpretive communities without losing focus on their own particular ends and purposes for interpreting Scripture. The same arguments Origen and others offer for engaging pagan philosophy in service of different Christian ends seem to work here equally well.

Reading the OT as Scripture is also rendered more complex because of the difficult but necessary relationship of the church to Israel, a relationship that Christians have sometimes tried to sunder, elide, or erase. This relationship also bears the scars of Christian violence against Jews. These scars should cast a cautionary shadow over all of our thinking about these matters, but should not stop us from thinking about them.

In addition to these caveats, there is also a host of specific interpretive issues relating to interpreting the Old Testament as part of Scripture that might require their own companion. Instead of trying to resolve these, I would like to focus on issues regarding reading the OT as Scripture that draw their force from two images for thinking about Christ's relationship to the law. The aim of this is to suggest that each of these ways of thinking about Christ in relation to the law tends to generate a certain type of reading practice with regard to the OT. Moreover, each image carries with it some possible unfortunate hermeneutical implications. Thus, I will try to present these images in ways that correct or foreclose some of their unfortunate hermeneutical implications. Although I think one of these paths is preferable to the other, I see no reason to reject either of these images and their attendant reading practices. In this way, I want to show that there are some characteristically Christian ways of reading the OT as Scripture, but there is little point in trying to reduce this diversity to a single interpretive proposal.

The two images I want to explore are 1) the claim that Christ is the subject matter or *res* of all Scripture including the OT, and 2) the notion that comes from Rom 10:4 that Christ is the end or *telos* of the law.

It would, of course, seem odd for a theologian to deny that as believers attend to the OT, these texts might in ways both conventional and figural direct believers' thoughts, loves, lives, and worship to Christ. Moreover, if one grants that this can happen in more and less immediate ways, there seems little point in arguing against such a claim. If this is what one means by claiming that Christ is the subject matter of the Old Testament then one can hardly find fault with the notion. At the same time, such a claim does not appear to require any particular interpretive practice.

The notion of Christ as subject matter of the OT becomes potentially problematic, however, when one takes it to indicate that there is something or someone lying hidden beneath the surface of the OT. This tends to generate interpretation as excavation. Indeed much modern scholarly biblical criticism operates on the assumption that there is something hidden by or hidden inside the text. Moreover, the corollary of this assumption is that the properly trained critic is just the right person both to determine what this subject matter is and how to extract it from the text. Although the precise digging tools will differ, the basic set of assumptions seems the same whether one is looking for Christ, or the suppressed voices of the marginal in Israelite society, or for the lost religious consciousness of ancient Israel. In addition, this type of interpretation seems designed to end interpretation, theological or otherwise. On this view, once you have located whatever has been buried within or hidden by the text, there seems to be little need for the text any longer. When interpretation is viewed as excavation and you have finished digging that hole and extracting the desired article, the text is just excess dirt; you have little need for it, except to excavate further for something else. Thus, I would argue that the best way to employ the idea of Christ as the subject matter of the OT is to keep the notion of subject matter so general or abstract that it simply recognizes that the OT can direct one's attention to

Christ in any number of ways and for a variety of purposes, none of which requires a specific interpretive method.

Turning to the idea that Christ is the end of the law, one also finds that there are pitfalls associated with this image. First, this notion can and has been used to underwrite the claim that the law is abolished. This takes *telos* in the sense of termination or cessation. This would seem directly counter to the ways in which Paul is arguing in Rom 9:30—10:4. Moreover, the idea that the law has somehow ceased raises rather sharp theological questions about the character of a God who would make everlasting promises in this law only later to terminate those promises with the coming of Christ.

Even if one does not opt for this rather flat-footed understanding of Christ being the end of the law, there are still other potentially problematic ways of reading the OT in the light of the claim that Christ is the end of the law. For example, we have Jesus's own claims to fulfill the law and the prophets (Matt 5:17), which would raise the question of the status of the law and prophets once their fulfillment has arrived. In addition, there are Paul's claims in Galatians 3. There one gets the very real impression that the law, at least understood in a very particular way, is no longer needed as a pointer to Christ once Christ has actually arrived on the scene; though in this case, Paul's use of the temporal priority of God's promise to Abraham, a promise found in the law, to trump promises to Moses indicates that something more complex is at work here. Thus, even in the light of Galatians 3, one should be careful about asserting that Paul thinks of the law as abolished in the light of the coming of Christ.

If the idea that Christ is the end of the law is to guide faithful Christian reading of the OT, then it will be important to think of *telos* here in terms of the goal toward which some movement or activity is directed. This seems to be what Paul has in mind in Romans as he struggles to answer the question of how Israel, who had the advantages of the law, which is holy, just, and good, as well as zeal, managed not to find what the Gentiles found without any of Israel's advantages. The key in 10:4 seems to lie in the fact that zeal in interpreting the law apart from knowledge of the *telos* of the law cannot bring a good result. Paul's point here would seem to be that the OT properly understood will lead you to its proper end or goal, that is, Christ. Such a view might work as a regulative assertion. Paul's own practice of reading the OT, however, makes it clear that he does not think that recognizing Christ as the *telos* of the law requires a single interpretive method.

This still leaves the question of what to do when the *telos* of the law is revealed. If the law, properly understood, reaches its goal in Christ, is the law still needed once Christ has been revealed? Is there a need for the OT in the light of the NT? One way of answering the various forms of this question is rightly to point out that even in the light of the NT the OT can be useful in filling out a richer, fuller picture of Christ. Although this retains the continued relevance of the OT for Christian readers, it does so primarily at the cost of keeping the OT as little more than interpretive background.

As a way of addressing this, one might expand the notion of Christ as the *telos* or goal of the law. Seeing Christ as the *telos* of the law makes best sense when one also sees that Christ is the *telos* or goal of the lives of believers. This goal is decisively known and recognized by believers in the present to such a degree that Christ as *telos* can provide a direction for the lives, thoughts, affections, and prayers of believers. At the same time, believers understand that there are significant respects in which they have not yet reached their final end.

Paul in Philippians 3 nicely illustrates this idea. In this chapter Paul contrasts a pattern of thinking, feeling, and acting that is driven by a confidence in the flesh with a pattern of thinking, feeling, and acting that is marked by friendship with the cross of Christ. As Paul lays these two patterns out, he notes that he was an excellent example of the first pattern. His catalogue of achievements narrated in vv. 4–6 displays his unparalleled devotion to the God of Israel. He displayed zeal so intense that he was willing to kill those he viewed as a threat to Judaism. Of course, this way of thinking, acting, and feeling was transformed in the light of Paul's encounter with the crucified and resurrected Christ. He now looks to "gain" Christ and to "be found" in him. Christ "grabs" Paul and in doing so becomes the *telos* of Paul's loves, thoughts, and actions. Apart from Christ's prior work it seems unlikely that Paul could come to read Christ as the *telos* of the law.

It is significant though that Paul recognizes he has not yet grabbed hold of Christ, his *telos*, with anything like the finality with which Christ first grabbed him. Instead, he presses on, reaches out, moves ahead in the confident hope that the God who began a good work in him (and the Philippians) will bring that work to completion at the day of Christ (1:6). Moreover, the fact that by 3:17 Paul urges the Philippians to imitate him suggests that he takes his own experience here to be normative and imitable.

Taking Christ as both the *telos* of the law and the *telos* of the Christian life provides an excellent, but by no means the only, regulative framework within which Christians can read the OT as Scripture. Such a framework does not require any particular interpretive method or practice. It can recognize that highly sophisticated historical analyses of a Psalm can under certain circumstances move believers ever closer to Christ. At the same time it can employ the same Psalm in worship so that the reading or chanting of the Psalm both points to Christ and directs believers to a deeper friendship with Christ.

Further, taking Christ as both the *telos* of the law and the *telos* of the Christian life retains the eschatological tension between the arrival of the law's *telos* with the life, death, and resurrection of Jesus, and that time when believers will truly grasp their final end. This tension means that the OT and the NT together will retain their role as God's providentially ordered vehicle to bring us to our final home, even after the law's *telos* has arrived.

Theological Interpretation of Scripture and Philosophical Hermeneutics

Long before the recent scholarly interest in theological interpretation, groups of biblical scholars and theologians displayed a deep interest in hermeneutics. In a general sense hermeneutics focuses on the conditions for human understanding. More particularly, hermeneutics concerns the theories of textual interpretation. Often the lines between these two notions of hermeneutics become blurry. It would be odd, of course, to develop and argue about theories of textual meaning, for example, without also making assumptions about human understanding. In addition, because of their own disciplines' close attachments to textual interpretation, literary theorists and philosophers have also devoted a great deal of attention to hermeneutics in both its general and its specific senses. To cover all of this adequately would go far beyond the confines of this companion. At the same time, I run the risk of failing to do justice to the great interdisciplinary sophistication and depth of hermeneutical scholarship produced by theologians and biblical scholars. This confession should encourage the student of theological interpretation to read and investigate widely in these areas.

Many of the theologians and some of the biblical scholars who work in hermeneutics do so because they have a deep interest in having the Bible play a role in the faith and life of Christians. Moreover, they share a concern that scriptural interpretation be orderly, rational, and defensible. This is not simply a theoretical concern either. The history of the church, particularly as its political power increased, is littered with incidents where Christians have invoked their interpretations of Scripture to underwrite appallingly sinful actions. Thus, one can understand a concern with textual meaning and hermeneutical rigor as part of a larger concern to combat or to foreclose the seemingly limitless potential of human sinfulness when it comes to interpreting and embodying Scripture. A concern with textual meaning reflects moral and theological desires to regulate Christians' scriptural interpretation and application and not simply philosophical interests.

In addition, this hermeneutical concern seeks to balance the theological conviction that Scripture is the word of God and the work of human hands. The fact that Scripture is the word of God invests scriptural interpretation with a particular importance. Further, that Scripture is the work of human authors can be taken to imply that the communicative intentions of these authors should be given a type of interpretive privilege.

If one's interpretive practice is governed by a general hermeneutical theory (of any type), then it is very hard to avoid the situation where theological interpretation of Scripture becomes the activity of applying theological concerns to interpretation done on other grounds. It seems all too easy to allow a general theory of textual meaning to provide the *telos* of theological interpretation. The key to interpreting theologically lies in keeping theological concerns and ends primary to all others. In this way, theology becomes a form of scriptural interpretation, not simply its result. Christians are called to interpret and embody Scripture as a way of advancing toward their proper ends in God. When Augustine spoke of Scripture as a vehicle to carry us to our true home, he was aware that we might find the vehicle so plush and the ride so smooth that we would forget we are on a journey and not a joy ride. We would end up loving the ride more than we desire to get to our destination. To resist that temptation, Christians need to be sure that our interpretations and embodiments of Scripture are always directed toward enhancing our prospects of reaching our true home.

There is a variety of scholarly works that address matters of theological interpretation through various hermeneutical approaches. No comments or criticisms I offer here should be a basis for keeping students from reading these works on their own. In what follows, however, I do want to offer some critical comments about several hermeneutical concerns and their relationship to theological interpretation of Scripture. I will comment on two particular areas: 1) the general relationship between theories of textual meaning and theological interpretation of Scripture, and 2) the place of authors and their intentions in theological interpretation. With regard to each of these issues, I will try to present the reasons such issues are relevant to theological interpretation and ways in which these issues appear differently in the light of the account of theological interpretation of Scripture offered above.

THEORIES OF TEXTUAL MEANING

There are two general points I wish to make about the theories of textual meaning. The first is a point that is internal to the ongoing quest for a general theory of textual meaning. It concerns the term "meaning" that lies at the heart of the matter.

Debates between proponents of various approaches to theological interpretation often end up focused on the issue of textual meaning. These arguments can often seem quite heated, perhaps even generating more heat than light. When that appears to be the case, it is likely that the term "meaning" in these debates is often required to stand in for a range of overlapping but often logically separable questions and concerns. In cases like this, making such separations clear can often help students discern where the real disagreements lie and how those disagreements might be resolved.

All of us, especially those of us who teach, use the verb "to mean" and the noun "meaning" numerous times each day in interactions with students, colleagues, and family members. As long as these interactions run smoothly, there is probably no reason to reflect on our use of "to mean" and "meaning." There are, however, significant times when we find ourselves studying, preaching, writing about, and attempting to order our faith and practice in the light of Scripture, that we run into conflicts. When faced with such conflicts, we get nowhere by simply saying, "The meaning of John 1:1 is x and not y." Such an assertion merely elicits the counter "No, the meaning of John 1:1 is y and not x." In such an argument one party may have the authority to impose a resolution to this disagreement, but that really puts a halt to rather than resolves a dispute.

If such a dispute is to be resolved, it will not happen by asserting x is the meaning of John 1:1 with a louder and deeper voice. We need a clearer picture of how the relevant parties are using the word "meaning" and the reasons they give for using the word in those ways rather than others. In fact, the better and more precise we can be about what we are doing in interpreting any particular text in a specific way in a concrete situation, the easier it will be to avoid using the term "meaning" to justify our interpretations. In this light, we should not be surprised, then, to find many of our interpretive disputes are resolved as it becomes clear that the various parties are actually doing different and not necessarily incompatible things when they interpret a particular text. In these cases the dispute ends because the parties are not actually arguing about the same things. The way forward in such situations is to become clearer and more articulate about the precise thing each party is seeking when it interprets a given text.

In those more difficult cases when it appears that various parties are interpreting the same texts with the same set of interpretive aims and still reaching different, incompatible results, such disputes can only move toward resolution by arguing further about what is to count as evidence, and how to evaluate that evidence. Recourse to the term "meaning" here will impede rather than enhance such movement. Thus, in those cases where we really have serious interpretive disagreements, the term "meaning" just gets in the way.

Let us return to the hypothetical argument about John 1:1 mentioned above. Each party seeks to interpret the phrase, "In the beginning was the word (*logos*)." In this dispute interpreter A relies on the verbal connections between the beginning of John's Gospel and Genesis 1:1. She also looks at the ways other Jews writing in Greek, such as Philo, use the term *logos*, noting both similarities and differences. She combines these findings with observations about the use of "word" in the OT and other relevant Hebrew literature, concluding that by calling Jesus the *logos* John seeks to connect Jesus with the "wisdom" of God, the rational principle that God employs in creation. Such usage is, at best, ambiguous regarding such things as Christ's divinity and pre-existence. On further matters about which John is ambiguous, interpreters might well be silent.

Interpreter B is mostly interested in bringing a Nicene notion of the relationships between the divine persons to bear on John 1:1 against any attempts to treat the Son as a created being. For her, John 1:1 (perhaps along with Phil 2:6–7) raises the issue of whether the Son is created or eternally begotten. Moreover, John 1:1 seems to raise questions about the singularity of God, a matter that passages such as Deut 6:4–5 seem to put beyond question. Interpreter B takes John 1:1 to pose issues that it does not itself resolve, issues that can only adequately be resolved in the light of Nicene dogma. Attempts to resolve these problems in other ways will result in inadequate accounts of the Christian God and raise serious doubts about the possibility of our salvation.

Interpreter A is concerned with interpreting John 1:1 through a historically plausible reconstruction of the text's conceptual and verbal antecedents in order to present what a late-first- or early-second-century reader, sufficiently aware of these antecedents, might have understood upon reading the phrase, "In the beginning was the word (*logos*)." Alternatively, B is concerned with interpreting John 1:1 in the light of later Christian theological developments, developments for which John 1:1 might be seen as a crucial catalyst.

Each of these interpretive options represents paths that real interpreters of John 1:1 have trod. Each can be evaluated on its own terms with regard to how they handle various pieces of evidence or in the light of new evidence. There may be good reasons why one might opt for one of these interpretive paths over another at any particular point in time. It is unclear, however, what is advanced by claiming that one of these paths leads to the "meaning" of John 1:1 and the other does not or cannot lead to "meaning."

The upshot of this all-too-brief discussion is that when faced with interpretive disagreement and debate, we are more likely to detect real points of disagreement and have a hope of resolving those disagreements if we withdraw claims about what must be the "meaning" of a text in favor of more detailed claims about what our specific interpretive aims are in particular cases. Thus, I am doubtful that we can develop a general theory of textual meaning that does not rely on question-begging accounts of meaning. Our actual interpretations will be much more clearly directed and our interpretive disputes much more open to resolution apart from the invocation of "meaning."

AUTHORS DIVINE AND HUMAN

As I noted above, those theological interpreters who are especially interested in hermeneutics bring the very significant concern that, this side of the reign of God, Christians need to be attentive to their own tendencies to read Scripture in ways that underwrite their sin. In addition to this concern, such interpreters also worry that without an agreed-upon hermeneutical standard against which to measure specific interpretations there will be no rational way to evaluate competing interpretations. In the worst-case scenario, interpreters become judges unto themselves; interpretive anarchy will reign.

The intention of any specific biblical text's human author provides one sort of hermeneutical standard that has garnered a good deal of scholarly support among theologians and biblical scholars. Those who advocate the author's intention as a regulative standard for interpretation have had to battle on two fronts: hermeneutical and theological. The battles have focused on just what is involved in displaying an author's intention and why such intentions should be normative. Hermeneutically and philosophically, notions of intention have become much more precise. I think the argument that such intentions should be theologically normative is much more problematic. It is much easier to argue that there is a reasonable way of thinking about and discerning an author's intention than to argue that displaying such intentions should be the primary focus of theological interpretation.

One of the major criticisms of attempts to display an author's intentions is that it presumes an account of human subjectivity that, while characteristic of the Enlightenment, is difficult to maintain today. That is, some ways of talking about authors assume that authors (like other humans) are fully (or substantially) autonomous and aware of themselves and their intentions. Further, it assumes that the texts authors write (or language more generally) are suitable vehicles for mediating those intentions from one autonomous self-aware mind to another. This notion of selfhood has come under sustained and vigorous attack from suspicious critics such as Marx, Nietzsche, and Freud (among others). Moreover, from a theological perspective, this account of human selfhood simply does not fit with a view that humans are created in the image of the triune God whose inner life is constituted by its relationships rather than by autonomy. Our creaturely status needs to circumscribe all notions of autonomy and freedom. Further, Christian convictions about sin and sin's manifestations in human habits of self-deception in thought, word, and deed should make Christians wary of any presumptions about humans being fully or substantially present to themselves. Short of the consummation of God's reign, we shall not know as fully as we are known by God. If, therefore, we are to reconstitute notions of authorial intention, we will need to do so in ways that do not presume that via an analysis of a text we can climb inside an author's head and share with the author an immediate and unfettered access to the author's intentions.

The best way to do this is to reshape the notion of intention so that it does not presume problematic notions of selfhood. One way to do this is to try to distinguish authorial motives from an author's communicative intentions.[12] "That

12. This distinction is initially made by Quentin Skinner (see "Motives, Intentions and the Interpretation of Texts"). For biblical

is to say, one ought to distinguish between *what* an author is trying to say (which might be called a 'communicative intention') and *why* it is being said (which might be called a motive)."[13] An author might write from any number of motives: a desire for fame and fortune, hopes of acquiring tenure, a deep psychological need for self-expression, etc. There may well be motives at work of which an author is not fully conscious. In order to uncover an author's motives, analysis of her texts is never enough. Moreover, a desire to uncover authorial motives will generally be very difficult to fulfill. In the case of ancient authors an interest in motives will be almost totally frustrated by our lack of information.

Alternatively, one need not attend to an author's motives in rendering an account of her communicative intentions. Instead, such an account requires attention to matters of semantics, of linguistic conventions operative at the time, and of implication and inference, to name just three. In dealing with biblical writers attention to these matters is inescapably historical. Indeed, in many respects the practices required to display an author's communicative intentions will be familiar to biblical critics even if they do not characterize their work as offering an account of an author's communicative intention.

Accounting for an author's communicative intention does not depend on having textually mediated access to an autonomous, aware, authorial self. In fact, in the case of the Bible, it probably does not require the identification of a specific historical character as an author. Rather, in the case of

---

scholars this notion is expertly articulated by Mark Brett (see "Motives and Intentions in Genesis 1"). In what follows I am largely indebted to Brett's work.

13. Brett, "Motives and Intentions in Genesis 1," 5.

Paul, for example, it depends on a knowledge of Greek and the linguistic conventions operative in the first century; an ability to detect and explicate allusions, indirect references, implications, and inferences; and a measure of familiarity with the set of social conventions of which letter writing is a part. The precise ways to mix and match all of these considerations will always be matters of argument and debate. For example, there is no set formula or method that will reveal when one should rely more heavily on semantics than on social conventions or on possible OT allusions. In fact, the great majority of interpretive arguments among biblical scholars can be cast as arguments about how to weigh and evaluate the role of these pieces of evidence. A great number of factors can determine the outcome of these arguments, but they are not dependent upon an accounting of Paul's motives even if we could know them.

Needless to say, these are always probability judgments, open to revision in the light of further evidence and argument. Given this measure of provisionality, which is the measure within which we generally have to operate, we can expect to make fairly confident claims about an author's communicative intention.

It is here in regard to establishing an author's communicative intention that my arguments overlap most closely with those who rely on speech-act theory. Like them, I recognize that all utterances are intelligible because they are contextually embedded and that successful communication relies on the knowledge and operation of linguistic and social conventions. To the extent that those who rely on speech-act theory recognize that one needs to make *ad hoc* arguments about the relative importance of specific conventional and contextual concerns in order to account for specific utterances, I would say that we both recognize the priority of practical reasoning in interpretation.

I would argue, however, that there are really two different trajectories in speech-act theory, or two ways of carrying forward the views laid out by J. L. Austin in *How to Do Things with Words*. Philosophers such as Richard Rorty and Jeffrey Stout treat Austin as a therapeutic philosopher, a philosopher who helps us eliminate problems and confusions. This way of reading Austin treats him as one of several philosophers and linguists who eliminate confusions about language by showing that words and utterances become intelligible because of the way they are used in context and in the light of various conventions, not because words have fixed meanings as inherent properties. This way of treating Austin places the emphasis on the priority of practical reasoning in interpretation.

The other way of carrying forward Austin's work is characterized by John Searle's attempt to use Austin's work to develop a philosophy of language and, at least implicitly, a metaphysic or ontology.[14] Kevin Vanhoozer casts Searle as Melancthon—speech-act theory's systematic theologian—to Austin's Luther.[15] Given this account, I would argue that Rorty, Stout, and I stand with Austin. Others such as Anthony Thiselton, Nicholas Wolterstorff, and Kevin Vanhoozer stand more with Searle. I am not persuaded that speech-act theory can provide either a theory of meaning or the basis for arguing for the interpretive priority of the communicative intention of authors.

14. Searle's key work here is *Speech Acts: An Essay in the Philosophy of Language*.

15. Vanhoozer, *Is There a Meaning*, 209.

Although I have indicated that the vast majority of biblical scholarship can be understood as an attempt to display the communicative intentions of biblical writers, I do not think this should be the primary or determinative consideration for theological interpretation of Scripture. Making the communicative intention of Scripture's human authors the primary goal of theological interpretation will unnecessarily and unfortunately truncate Christians' abilities to read Scripture theologically in several important respects. For example, although Christians will want to employ a variety of reading strategies with regard to the OT, they will certainly want to read passages such as Isa 7:14 and 11:1–5 as references to Christ. In addition, Christians will want to interpret John 1 and Phil 2:6–11 in the light of Nicene dogma. It seems extremely unlikely that our best approximation of the communicative intention of Isaiah, John, or Paul will address these matters. If an author's communicative intention is the primary aim of theological interpretation, these particular interpretive options will become, at best, subsidiary matters. Alternatively, it seems highly likely that the communicative intention of the writer of Ps 137:7–9 reflects a longing to see the children of his enemies thrown against stones. If theological interpretation as a rule makes authorial intention its aim, then it not only will have a difficult time accounting for christological and Trinitarian readings of the NT, it may also end up supporting unchristian dispositions and actions.

Thomas Aquinas, for one, clearly recognized this difficulty. Writing in the middle part of the 13th century, Aquinas may be best known to students as a systematic theologian or even as a philosophical theologian. This characterization certainly reflects aspects of Aquinas's work. First, however,

Aquinas was by profession a teacher and commentator upon Scripture and a theological interpreter of Scripture. The foundation for Aquinas's scriptural interpretation was the "literal sense" (*sensus literalis*) of Scripture. For Aquinas, the literal sense of Scripture is what the author intends. Thomas holds that the author of Scripture is God, or more precisely, the Holy Spirit. The human authors under the Spirit's inspiration are significant though secondary in this respect. The Spirit is capable of understanding all things and intending more by the words of Scripture than humans could ever fully grasp. This means that believers should not be surprised to find that there may be many manifestations of the literal sense of a passage. Here is what Thomas says in the *Summa Theologiae*: "Since the literal sense is what the author intends, and since the author of Holy Scripture is God, Who by one act comprehends everything all at once in God's understanding, it is not unfitting as Augustine says [*Confessions* XII], if many meanings are present even in the literal sense of a passage of Scripture" (*Summa Theologiae* 1.Q.1 art. 10). This notion of authorial intention, which is very different from the modern hermeneutical account of authors mentioned above, will allow someone to treat christological interpretations of Isaiah as the literal sense of that text without disallowing other more historical accounts of the literal sense of Isaiah. Moreover, such an approach will allow Christians to treat Psalm 139 in ways that do not invite Christians to pray for revenge on their enemies. Thus, such an approach will keep theological concerns primary in theological interpretation rather than making theological concerns subsidiary to hermeneutical concerns.

Thus far, I have addressed ways of thinking about theological interpretation of Scripture that place hermeneutical concerns at the forefront. These concerns are, for the most part, driven by a serious concern to regulate Christians' proclivities to sinfulness and self-deception in their biblical interpretation. There are several issues internal to this practice that I have tried to raise briefly in the material above. In addition, although this is not a sufficient reply, it is important to note that the biblical bases for Apartheid were provided by scholars of the Dutch Reformed Church in South Africa and that several German scholars, most famously Gerhard Kittel, were Nazi sympathizers. Thus, scholarly rigor cannot guarantee faithful interpretation.

Most importantly, however, I have tried to point out that there is a theological cost to be paid in letting hermeneutical concerns play a normative role in theological interpretation.

Rather than rely on hermeneutics to combat interpretive anarchy and sinful interpretation, believers should seek to regulate these tendencies ecclesially. In short, we should not ask philosophy to do the church's work. Scripture is primarily addressed to communities and it is within Christian communities that believers are to be formed and transformed in ways that enhance their movement into ever deeper communion with God and each other.

The practice of theological interpretation is, at its core, an activity of Christian communities. The triune God, to whom scriptural texts bear witness, calls us into such communities. Hence, Christian communities provide the contexts whereby we learn, as the body of Christ through the power of the Holy Spirit, to interpret and embody Scripture in ways that enhance rather than frustrate our communion with God and others.

Instead of relying on ever-more-sophisticated hermeneutical theories, Christian communities need to provide an alternative regulative structure that will combat our manifest tendencies to interpret Scripture in ways that lead us into sin. There are two central components to this regulative structure. The first concerns the role of the body of Christ in admonishing and correcting one another. Of course, Paul repeatedly displays this in his epistles, admonishing and correcting communities with whom he is deeply connected. Moreover, Paul expects these communities to do this corrective work themselves. In the case of the Corinthians for example, it is sometimes hard to discern whether Paul is more frustrated by the various escapades of believers in Corinth or by their manifest inability to be self-aware and self-correcting.

If believers are to admonish and correct one another without tearing each other apart they will need to have a number of conversational habits well established. They will need large measures of openness and accountability to each other as well. I will speak a bit more about these matters in the next chapter.

Practices of forgiveness and reconciliation provide the second crucial component that Christian communities rely on to regulate our tendencies to interpret Scripture in ways that lead us into sin. There are simply no guarantees (with or without a hermeneutical method) that Christians can counter their tendencies to interpret Scripture in ways that underwrite or lead to sin. For believers, however, their sin need not be the last word on any matter. The community comprised of Jesus's followers is formed through the direct instruction of Jesus, through their prayer, and through their worship to forgive just as God has forgiven them. Moreover, they seek to bear witness through word and deed to the God who is reconciling all things in Christ.

Although more needs to be said about these communal practices, I hope that I have said enough here to indicate that the ecclesial contexts in which theological interpretation of Scripture finds its proper home also provides adequate means of dealing with sinful and failed interpretation apart from a rigorous hermeneutical method.

QUESTIONS

1. What is the end or *telos* of the Christian life?

2. How is the end of the Christian life connected to theological interpretation?

3. What is the Rule of Faith and what role might it play in theological interpretation?

4. How do Christians understand the relationship between Old and New Testaments?

5. Is it important for theological interpretation to develop a theory of textual meaning?

THREE

Practices and Habits of Theological Interpretation

It is now time to address more concretely some of the practices constitutive of a form of theological interpretation of
Scripture that flows from the account of Scripture given in
chapter 1 and that seeks to keep theological and ecclesiological concerns primary in contrast to the approaches discussed
in chapter 2. For the most part, the practices and habits discussed here are interconnected. It is difficult to practice one
of these well without also succeeding in the others. Of course,
problems in one area will tend to generate problems in other
areas. It is in the same way difficult to discuss one practice
or habit in isolation from the others, and there is no obvious
place to start. I will begin with several interpretive practices
and habits that stand in contrast to those discussed above and
then move to examine some ecclesial habits and practices.
First, I look at the importance of the pre-modern interpretation and then the importance of figural reading.

ATTENDING TO PRE-MODERN INTERPRETATION

As I indicated at the beginning of chapter 2, pre-modern
biblical interpreters read Scripture in the light of its role in
bringing believers to their proper end in God. They also kept

theological and ecclesial concerns primary in their scriptural interpretation. Scripture was an indispensible gift from God that enabled them to understand and order the world in which they lived and moved and worshipped. I also indicated how and why this situation changed in the modern period.

If the type of theological interpretation advocated here is to flourish in the present, it will require contemporary believers to relearn the habits and practices that constituted a flourishing pattern of theological interpretation in the past.[1] I am not advocating a recreation of the past in the present, as if that were possible. There is no point in engaging in wistful longing for a lost golden age of theological interpretation.

Alternatively, when a practice is in good working order we should normally expect that subsequent generations will build upon and advance the successes of the past, while seeking to avoid and correct its errors. Of course, those things that will count as successes and errors will not always be evident to us; it may take some time before one can discern the difference between success and error. Such discernment will always require argument and debate over time. Thus, if we are aiming to reinvigorate a practice like theological interpretation, those eager to succeed in the present can only hope to do so in the light of the successes of the past.

Most importantly, with regard to pre-modern interpretation it is important to recall that Christians see themselves as part of an ongoing, historically and geographically extended, and culturally diverse communion of saints. The saints are those who have masterfully performed the Scriptures, those who have allowed their engagements with Scripture to

1. See O'Keefe and Reno, *Sanctified Vision.*

draw them into an ever deeper communion with God and neighbor. If these are also the ends of theological interpretation in the present, then it is unclear why one would seek to engage Scripture with these same ends in mind without also attending to the lives and interpretations of such successful practitioners. Although we cannot know in advance which pre-modern interpretations will be most important for any particular situation, it should also be clear that attention to such work has an important role to play in the reinvigoration and maintenance of theological interpretation.

FIGURAL READING

The second consideration that will be important if theological concerns are to retain their priority in the theological interpretation of Scripture has to do with the importance of figural reading. Figural reading is a practice that is integral to Jewish and Christian reading of their respective Scriptures. It is common to contrast figural interpretations with the "literal sense" of Scripture. In speaking about the literal sense of a scriptural text above, I stressed already that the "literal sense," does not precisely correspond to our modern notions of "literal." Moreover, there are significant debates around how Christians have defined (and should define) the "literal sense" of Scripture. For now, let me propose the following working notion of the "literal sense" of Scripture. Others may want to challenge this, but this is an account that also would have a large number of supporters among theologians past and present. Let us take the "literal sense" of a passage to be the meanings conventionally ascribed to a passage by Christian communities. Thus, the literal sense will be those meanings

Christians regularly ascribe to a passage in their ongoing struggles to live and worship faithfully before the triune God. This means that the literal sense of Scripture will be those interpretations Christians take to be primary, the basis and norm for all subsequent ways of interpreting the text. Let us consider this famous example from Isaiah: "Behold, a young woman (virgin) will conceive and bear a child and you shall call him Immanuel" (Isa 7:14). If this verse is read in the context of Isaiah, it seems pretty clear that the child in question here is the son born to Isaiah of Jerusalem as noted in Isa 8:1–3. It is equally clear that Matthew and the Christian tradition generally take this verse to be a prophetic announcement of the coming birth of Jesus almost 750 years later. Christians can grant that both of these are the literal sense of Isaiah. This is because the God who inspires these words is perfectly able to make them refer to both these characters. This is, in part, what Aquinas was referring to when he spoke of the possibility of there being many literal senses of the same passage.

If we use this working definition of the literal sense, then figural interpretations will use a variety of interpretive techniques to extend the literal sense of Scripture in ways that enhance Christians' abilities to live and worship faithfully in the contexts in which they find themselves. If we must relearn how to use Scripture as the basis for ordering and comprehending the world to revive theological interpretation, then we must also recognize that there will be times when the literal sense of Scripture may not offer us a sharp enough vision to account for the world in which we live. In those cases, we will need to read Scripture figuratively.

Let me offer an example of figural interpretation as a way of explaining this further. Christians in America will be intensely aware of the fractured nature of the church. It often seems like hardly a week goes by without there being news of a denomination or a church being rent by arguments over human sexuality, abortion, just war, or the color of the carpet in the sanctuary.

I do not have the space to explore all of the hows and whys of church division. It is, however, very easy to offer accounts of church division that mirror accounts of our current political divisions, using language such as "liberal and conservative" or even "red and blue." Describing church division in this or any other way will at the same time decisively shape the way one tries to live in the light of those divisions and what solutions one will seek. The way one diagnoses the problem will shape where one looks for a cure.

Here, as a way of illustrating the nature and importance of figural reading, I want to look at some scriptural passages which might provide Christians with ways of describing, thinking theologically and faithfully about, and living in the light of divisions within Christ's one body.

First, we need to note that the problems of a divided church are not really the same problems as those faced by Catholics and the various Reformers of the 16th century. Rather, the problems of a divided church as we know it today are really the result of ecumenism. In the 16th century, Lutherans, for example, did not represent a division within the church; they simply were not part of the church. The more Catholics and non-Catholics recognize each other as true Christians, the greater the problem of their division, the sharper the pain of this fracture.

If Christians today are to think about this theologically and scripturally we need to begin by recognizing that the New Testament will be of very limited use here. The NT has, for example, some things to say about divisions within the Corinthian church, but those are not at all of the same nature and scope as we face today. Indeed, if we are to find scriptural lenses for viewing contemporary church divisions, I suggest that we begin by turning to the OT. If interpreted figurally, biblical Israel and her divisions may provide us with ways of thinking and living in our own divided churches.[2]

Rather than see Israel's division into Northern and Southern Kingdoms as some sort of climactic event, passages like Psalm 106 and Jeremiah 3 lead us to view Israel's division as one of the results of Israel's persistent resistance to the Spirit of God. Division is simply one manifestation of this resistance, along with such things as grumbling against God and Moses in the wilderness, lapses into idolatry when Israel occupies the land, and the request for a human king. Interestingly, each of these manifestations of resistance becomes a form of God's judgment on Israel.

Let me explain this a bit more. Take the example of Israel's request for a human king in 1 Samuel 8. Although Samuel takes this as a personal affront, God makes it clear that it is simply part of a pattern of Israel's rejection of God's dominion, which has carried on from the moment God led the Israelites out of Egypt. This rejection of God results in the granting of a king. The granting of this request becomes the form of God's judgment on Israel as kings become both oppressively acquisitive and idolatrous (cf. 1 Sam 8:10–18; 12:16–25).

2. Those familiar with Ephraim Radner's powerful but difficult book *The End of the Church*, will recognize that I am both deeply indebted to Radner's figural reading, yet also differ from it in important ways. For what follows see also Fowl, "Theological and Ideological Strategies."

We see here that one of the forms of God's judgment is giving us what we want. If we treat division in this light it becomes clear that division is both a sign that we are willing to—and even desire to—live separate from our brothers and sisters in Christ, and it is also God's judgment upon that desire. Our failure to love, especially to love our brothers and sisters with whom we are at odds, lies at the root of our willingness and desire for separation. This separation in the form of church division is God's judgment on our failure to love as Christ commands.

One of the byproducts of Israel's resistance to God's Spirit is that their senses become dulled so that they are increasingly unable to perceive the workings of God's Spirit. Isaiah makes this particularly clear in 6:10; 28:9; 29:9–13. If one knows the prophetic literature well, one will recognize that this sort of stupefaction and blindness is a precursor to judgment. At those times when Israel is most in need of hearing God's word and repenting, they have also rendered themselves least able to hear that word. Judgment, however, leads to restoration. Importantly, passages such as Jeremiah 3 and Ezekiel 39 see restoration in terms of a unified Israel. This restored, unified Israel is so attractive and compelling that the nations are drawn to God because of what they see God doing for and with Israel (Isa 2:1–4). This blessing of the nations fulfills God's purposes in initially calling Abraham out from among his own people.

If we read the divided church in the light of biblical Israel and its division, then we face several conclusions: Division is one particularly dramatic way of resisting the Spirit of God. Such resistance further dulls our senses so that we are less able to discern the movements and promptings of God's

Spirit. Thus we become further crippled in reading/hearing God's word. The response called for throughout the prophets to this phenomenon is repentance. Whether our senses are so dulled that we cannot discern the proper form of repentance, whether God's judgment is so close at hand that we cannot avoid it, we cannot say. Instead, we are called to repent and to hope in God's unfailing plan of restoration and redemption in Christ.

The second set of scriptural texts we might look at are those NT passages that deal with unbelieving Israel. Romans 9–11 comes immediately to mind. It seems to me there is a right way and a wrong way to read our current divisions in the light of this passage. The wrong way is to devote time and energy to figuring out which part of the divided church is the natural vine, which parts are the grafted in, and which are cut off. Instead, we should remember that the God who grafts in also can lop off. There is no place for presumption or complacency here. Instead, we should, in and through our divisions, try to provoke our divided brothers and sisters through ever greater works of love to return to the vine. If I may quote Cardinal Ratzinger (now Benedict XVI) here, "Perhaps institutional separation has some share in the significance of salvation history which St. Paul attributes to the division between Israel and the Gentiles—namely that they should make 'each other envious,' vying with each other in coming closer to the Lord (Rom 11:11)."[3]

In each of these passages we see some of the consequences of church division for believers: Division is seen as a form of resistance to the Spirit of God. It dulls believers'

3. Ratzinger, *Church Ecumenism and Politics*, 87.

abilities to hear and respond to both the Spirit and the word, which, in turn, generates further unrighteousness. Division provokes God's judgment and is not part of God's vision for the restoration of the people of God. While both presumption and complacency are real temptations, neither is an appropriate response to division. Rather, we are called to sustained forms of repentance, "vying with each other in coming closer to God" with the aim of drawing the other to God. In the final passage I want to examine the consequences of church division for the world. In this case I want to look at Ephesians.

At the beginning of the epistle we are told that God's plan for the fullness of time is that all things shall be gathered together under Christ's lordship. Just as God's restoration of Israel brings a reunion of the divided Israel and the infusion of Gentiles, so in Christ, God will bring all things together in their proper relationship to Christ. It is important to note that this includes those principalities and powers that are not yet under Christ's dominion (1:10).

For Paul's purposes, the paramount activity of Christ's gathering of all things is the unification of Jews and Gentiles in one body through the cross and resurrection of Jesus. Ephesians 2 focuses on just this activity by which those near and those far off are brought together into one. This is and always has been God's providential plan for the redemption of the world. Paul calls this plan the "mystery which was made known to me by revelation" (3:2). It is, in short, the good news Paul has been commissioned to proclaim. Then in 3:9–10 he makes a claim upon which I want to focus. Paul is reflecting on his commission to proclaim this gospel of the unification of Jew and Gentile in Christ. He claims that God has given him the charge "to make everyone see what is the plan of the mystery hidden for ages in God who created all things: so that through the church the riches of God's wisdom might be made known to the principalities and powers in the heavenlies." The church, by its very existence as a single body of Jews and Gentiles united in Christ, makes God's wisdom known to the principalities and powers. As it appears here in Ephesians, the church's witness to the principalities and powers is integrally connected to, and may even depend upon, its unity.

What do we make of this in the light of our current situation of division? The most extreme way of putting the matter is to say that the church's witness to the principalities and powers is falsified or undermined by division. At the very least, one must say that the church's witness to the principalities and powers is hindered and frustrated by division.

Here, then, are a variety of scriptural passages that help us to understand and speak theologically about church division. This variety requires different styles of figural reading. Israel and its resistance to the Spirit becomes a figure of the church to call the divided church to repentance. The reading of Romans expands on this to provide some admonitions by way of analogy about how to live in a divided church. Finally, Ephesians implicitly warns of some of the consequences of division for the world at large, especially the principalities and powers. There is much more to say here if one were to develop this account further. I have merely tried to indicate how figural reading might look today as it extends the literal sense of various passages in order to help Christians perceive, order, and understand their current divided state.

ECCLESIAL PRACTICES

In the previous section I tried to show how reading Scripture figurally might open new ways for Christians to describe, think about, and, thereby, respond to church division. One might reply that this is all well and good, but is it not the case that scriptural interpretation is actually the cause of divisions within the church? It is very tempting to think that differences over Scripture and its interpretation and embodiment lie at the very heart of church division. Was it not, after all, Luther's insistence on Scripture alone (*sola scriptura*) that was the catalyst in his disputes with Rome? On several levels, the answer here must be no.

First, Luther's approach to Scripture was much more like than opposed to his late medieval contemporaries. Luther read the OT christologically, he relied on figural interpretation, and although he spoke of the clarity of Scripture, he did not assume that one could simply read Scripture apart from being formed to do so within the church.

Regardless of the rectitude of Luther's interpretations it is simply not possible to attribute the divisions within the post-Reformation church to Luther's deviation from an agreed-upon approach to and interpretation of Scripture. From the moment Scripture gets written down Christians, like Jews before them, have discussed, debated, and disagreed with each other about how to interpret and embody Scripture in the various contexts in which they found themselves. Short of that time when we know just as fully as we have been known, and until God's law is written directly on our hearts, Christians will continue to disagree, debate, and discuss matters of Scripture.

There is a variety of reasons for this. As followers of Christ we are called to a lifelong engagement with Scripture. Learning, knowing, and embodying Scripture is not a one-time achievement, but a life's work. Moreover, the contexts in which we struggle to live Scripture are always changing. Hence, a faithful interpretation in one context may not suffice in a different context. Finally, Scripture itself invites and sustains a chorus of interpretive voices. Luther was not the first Christian to have substantial disagreements with other Christians over scriptural interpretation. One need only look at the letters between Augustine and Jerome, or Theodore of Mopsuestia's account of Origen, just to name two famous examples. In a relatively few number of cases do Christians actually tear the body of Christ apart over scriptural interpretation.

I would like to suggest that when such divisiveness occurs in debates over Scripture it is not so much an issue of scriptural interpretation as the result of a separation of scriptural interpretation from a variety of other practices. These are the practices needed to keep the body of Christ whole in the midst of the inevitable debate, discussion, and argument that is part of the Christian community's ongoing engagement with Scripture. Moreover, as I indicated in chapter 2, these practices, rather than a philosophical hermeneutic, provide the regulative tools that Christians can use to keep their scriptural interpretation from leading them into sin. At this point I would like briefly to examine and reflect upon some of these ecclesial practices.

This will by no means be an account of all of the ecclesial practices relevant to theological interpretation of Scripture. I am not sure I know all of the relevant practices. These, however, seem to be rather important. Before I speak of practices, however, I must note again that all of these practices presume and are held together by love, by the love Christ has for believers and which Christ commands believers to have for each other. All church division is fundamentally a failure of love. All division proceeds from believers assuming that they are better off apart from each other than together. Division is a contradiction of ecclesial love,[4] especially love of our enemies within Christ's body. Doctrinal or scriptural differences cannot divide the church unless there is this prior failure of love. Further, scriptural interpretation cannot lead Christians into sin unless there is this prior failure of love.

Truth Seeking/Telling

Truth seeking and truth telling in Christ must be towards the top of any list of practices crucial to interpreting and embodying Scripture in the one body of Christ. On the one hand, this seems obvious. Debates, discussions, and arguments about Scripture or anything else cannot be life-giving apart from issues of truthfulness. On the other hand, those of us who still bear the lacerations or scars from having had brothers or sisters "speak the truth to us in love" will recognize how awful and divisive such "truth telling" can be. This sort of truth telling is often a thin disguise for personal hostility. If truth telling is to be a practice essential to keeping Christians' arguments about Scripture from leading them into sin or division, we will need to think of truth telling in christological terms.

Here is a brief account of what that might mean. In a passage filled with military images, the apostle Paul com-

4. See again Radner, *The End of the Church*.

mands us to bring every thought captive in obedience to Christ (2 Cor 10:5). It is not that Christ aims to obliterate all thoughts. Rather, they will be subjected to Christ's penetrating, healing gaze. Bringing all thoughts captive to Christ is a way of establishing or restoring their right relationship to the one who is the Truth. For example, think of the risen Christ's engagement with Peter around a charcoal fire in Galilee (John 21). Peter's deceit and betrayal is purged and he is restored in the course of being questioned by the resurrected one who is feeding him at the same time he interrogates him. The truth about Peter is never glossed. Nevertheless, the resurrected Christ uses this truth to transform Peter.

I mention truth telling first among the ecclesial practice for two related reasons. The first reason is that truth is the first casualty of sin. This, of course, makes it much more difficult to recognize sin, our own sin in particular. The second reason is that truth telling is the first component of the practices of forgiveness and reconciliation. I want to turn to these practices as essential for theological interpretation of Scripture.

Repentance, Forgiveness, and Reconciliation

To engage in the communal discussion, argument, and debate crucial to faithful embodiment of Scripture without fracturing or corrupting Christ's body, we must be capable of recognizing and naming sin, particularly our own sinfulness. This ability to recognize and name sin is not a one-time achievement, but an ongoing process of transformation and repentance. Recall that Luther began his ninety-five theses as follows: "When our Lord and Master, Jesus Christ, said 'Repent,' he called for the entire life of believers to be one of repentance." Without a community who is well practiced in the asking for and the offering of forgiveness, and without a community committed to the penitential work of reconciliation, we have little reason to recognize, much less repent of, our sin. If we think that sin is both the first *and last* word on our lives, then self-deception will always appear the easiest and best option.

When Christians' convictions about sin and their practices of forgiveness and reconciliation become distorted or inoperative, then Christians will also find that they cannot discuss, interpret, and embody Scripture in ways that will build up rather than tear apart the body of Christ. Rather than shaping and being shaped by faithful life and worship, our debates around Scripture will tend to fragment us.

A community whose common life is marked by the truthfulness of Christ and regularly engaged in practices of forgiveness and reconciliation will be able to engage in the discussion, argument, and debate crucial to interpret and embody Scripture faithfully in ways that build up rather than tear apart the body of Christ. In the absence of these practices Christians cannot expect that any hermeneutical theory will keep their scriptural interpretation from leading them into various sinful practices. Indeed, the fact that so many of the church's sinful practices in the modern era received the support of some of the most sophisticated scholars bears ample testimony to this fact.

Patience

I want to mention just one more practice crucial to engaging Scripture without dividing the body. This is patience. As a way of teasing out some issues around patience I want to focus on what I had often taken to be almost a throw-away line in Paul's letter to the Philippians. In 3:15 Paul wraps up a long plea to the Philippians to adopt a pattern of thinking, feeling, and acting that is focused around the patterns displayed to them by the crucified and resurrected Christ (2:5–11). This pattern of thinking, feeling, and acting will lead the Philippians to do certain things and to avoid other things, all of which Paul lays out in some detail. Adopting this pattern of thinking, feeling, and acting will enhance the Philippians' prospects of attaining their true end in Christ. Paul then turns to himself. He does not claim that he has attained this end yet. Rather, he presses on to the finish line so that he might win the prize of the heavenly call of God in Christ Jesus. These are some of the most elevated lines in the entire New Testament. Rather than stopping there and moving on to something else, Paul adds, "If any of you are inclined to adopt a different pattern of thinking, feeling, and acting, God will reveal to you the proper mindset to adopt." After this impassioned plea, Paul seems willing to allow that others may think differently. This is not because Paul is a good liberal and thinks that in matters of faith people should be allowed their own opinions. Rather, he can display a certain detachment from his own argument because he is convinced that God is directing and enabling the advancement of the gospel (cf.1:12–18). Paul does not have to coerce the Philippians into adopting his pattern of thinking, feeling, and acting because he is confident that God will bring both him and the Philippians to their proper end in Christ (1:6). It is this steadfast conviction about God's providence that enables Paul to be patient when the result he seeks is not immediately achieved.

Of course, patience should not be confused with passivity or apathy. Neither of these was characteristic of Paul. Just the sort of patience he reveals here in Philippians, however, displays a further ecclesial practice essential for theological interpretation. Like Paul, Christians can engage in serious and passionate argument over scriptural interpretation and its embodiment while at the same time manifesting a detachment over the results of those arguments in the hopeful expectation that the God who began a good work in them and their brothers and sisters will bring that good work to its proper end in God's own way at the day of Christ.

As I indicated above, these are by no means the only ecclesial practices on which Christians must rely as they interpret Scripture theologically. Rather than develop a comprehensive list, I have discussed these as a way of pointing out some of the differences between a way of characterizing theological interpretation in terms of a philosophical hermeneutic, on the one hand, and a manner of theological interpretation that seeks to ensure that Christians interpret Scripture theologically in the light of their ultimate end in God, on the other hand.

QUESTIONS

1. Why should theological interpreters pay attention to premodern scriptural interpretation?

2. What is "figural reading" and why is it important?

3. How might various aspects and practices of a church's common life be related to theological interpretation?

FOUR

Prospects and Issues for the Future

In the introduction to this volume I warned that this chapter may prove to be the most idiosyncratic piece of the companion. Here I will lay out what I take to be some of the future tasks and issues that theological interpreters of Scripture will need to engage in the years to come.

I will begin with what I take to be the least idiosyncratic concern. That is, we need to see more actual theological interpretation of Scripture. During the past couple of decades scholars have put forward a variety of more or less theoretical proposals arguing in different ways for the importance of interpreting Scripture theologically. These works in their own ways have helped to clear a space (primarily within the academy) where theological interpretation can take place in rigorous and scholarly fashion. Now the challenge is to see if such a space can be filled with high-quality interpretive work.

This will be more difficult than it might appear. It is really not sufficient simply to admonish people to do more actual theological interpretation. There are severe impediments to doing this well.

First, the separations between theology and biblical study have been so severe for so long that there are few scholars who have much experience interpreting theologically. The two commentary series currently devoted to interpreting various biblical books theologically are so far quite different in the sort of work they have generated. This is neither surprising nor a problem in the short term. One series is primarily written by those who would be identified as biblical scholars.[1] The other relies almost exclusively on theologians.[2]

Although these series are welcome additions and significant first steps, the next steps will be to have more cross-fertilization, more interpretive argument between theologians and biblical scholars, and more blurring of the lines between them. The best sign of significant progress in this regard will be when it is no longer acceptable to begin a criticism of a theological interpretation by saying, "I am not a biblical scholar, but . . ." or "I am not a theologian, but . . ."

To achieve real success here, however, there will need to be significant changes in the shape of graduate education so that the formation of new scholars does not happen through the standard divisions of theology and biblical studies. These changes will not happen quickly, but one hopeful sign is the inauguration of a ThD program at Duke Divinity School to run alongside the PhD program in the Religion Department.

In addition to changes in curricula and formation of graduate students, churches will need to do more in forming theological interpreters. Currently, in the US, the academy does most of the formative work for scholars. If, as I have argued above, theological interpretation of Scripture is a task best done in that community known as the church, guided and regulated by the church's convictions and practices, then churches need to get more actively involved both in forming

1. The Two Horizons New Testament Commentary.
2. Brazos Theological Commentary on the Bible.

theological interpreters and in developing the common life and practices that will allow them to play their proper regulative role. This will need to involve local congregations, judicatories, and ecclesial institutions. Apart from a much more significant and substantive ecclesial engagement in these issues, theological interpretation will continue primarily to reflect the concerns and the formative power of the academy. Church and academy need not be at war or even hostile to each other. Churches, however, cannot continue to cede so much formative control over to scholars in the academy and then employ those scholars in the expectation that they will easily be able to contribute to the formation of theological interpreters of Scripture for the churches' own ends and purposes.

A second, related issue concerns the formats or modes for carrying out theological interpretation. Even a cursory study of patristic and medieval interpretive practice will show that the sermon is one of the primary exemplars of theological interpretation in the pre-modern period. This is hardly surprising given the ecclesial contexts of pre-modern theological interpretation. Currently, the commentary and the scholarly article or monograph are the primary modes for contemporary theological interpretation. A challenge for the future of theological interpretation concerns how and in what ways sermons can become a mode for serious scholarly theological interpretation. In this light, it is commendable that in their edited volume, *The Art of Reading Scripture*, Ellen Davis and Richard Hays conclude the book with six of their own selected sermons.

Finally, after participating for fifteen or more years in debates and arguments over theological interpretation, I am beginning to wonder if some of the current arguments over methods and theories arise more from confessional differences than methodological differences. Again, this is not all that surprising. One might well expect that formation within a particular ecclesial tradition would then influence one's approach to theological interpretation in a variety of ways. In the same light, one would not want to reduce theoretical or methodological disagreements to confessional differences. Moreover, it would be difficult and perhaps unwise to seek to separate the confessional from the methodological too sharply. At the moment, however, there does not seem to be any easy way to bring these confessional differences into the arguments over methods of theological interpretation. Robert Wall has started to do some of this from a Weslyan perspective, but there is still a great deal left to do.[3]

It is easy to imagine how this could be done in ways that simply shut down rather than illumine debates. Indeed, one of the standard arguments in favor of historical criticism is that it provided a language and a forum within which scholars from different or no religious or confessional background could meet on neutral ground to study and to argue about biblical texts. Of course, the fragmentation of professional biblical studies in the light of various post-modern critiques has indicated that historical criticism was never really a neutral forum.[4] Thus, if theological interpreters are to bring issues of confessional difference into their discussions, as I think they

3. See Wall, "Reading the Bible from within Our Traditions"; Wall, "Facilitating Scripture's Future Role among Wesleyans"; and Robinson and Wall, *Called to Be Church*.

4. Michael Legaspi's critique of John Collins makes this point well. See Legaspi, "What Ever Happened to Historical Criticism?"

must, the first step will be to begin to develop conversational habits and dispositions that will enable this to happen in ways that enhance rather than frustrate conversation.

It may be that the ecumenical discussions of the past decades, despite their lack of concrete success in re-unifying churches, will provide some useful models for theological interpreters who want to explore the ways in which various Christian confessions might shape and be shaped by the practice of theological interpretation.

QUESTION

1. What have been the most important things that have formed you as an interpreter of Scripture?
2. What habits and dispositions do you think will help enhance conversations in which confessional differences arise?

FIVE

Guests at a Party

I began this companion using the image of the current state of theological interpretation as a chaotic party to which I was inviting you as my guest. For the most part I have spent the intervening pages describing a set of issues and concerns related to theological interpretation as I see things. I do not think this description is either arbitrary or idiosyncratic. Nevertheless, there are numerous others who are equally engaged in these issues, who see things differently from me, and who rightly emphasize other and alternative views. As a way of bringing this companion to a close, I want to introduce some of these fellow travelers and their works. I will do this by way of an annotated bibliography thematically rather than alphabetically organized.[1]

Before doing this I want to make several points as clear as I can. First, no one should take my annotations on these works as a suitable substitute for reading these works themselves. Secondly, this is only a partial listing. This is so for a

---

1. The lists of works for the scholars mentioned below seek to offer a fairly full accounting of any particular scholar's work in this area. I have not read all of these volumes, but I think students will benefit from having them listed here. I am particularly grateful to Chris Spinks for his work in filling out these lists.

variety of reasons. Space considerations impose one sort of limit on who can be included here. Organizing matters thematically will no doubt mean that certain scholars, who do not easily fit into one of these themes, may get left out. Finally, my vision of things is necessarily truncated. Thus, I apologize in advance to those whom I have left out for one reason or another. In the bibliography below, I will give full citations of the relevant works. Those works referred to directly in the body of the previous chapters will be included in the Works Cited pages.

Hermeneutics and Theological Interpretation

Although he does not figure as directly in current discussions about theological interpretation of Scripture, **Anthony Thiselton** has played an enormous role in bringing discussions of philosophical hermeneutics to bear on biblical studies. The two most important works in this regard are *The Two Horizons: New Testament Hermeneutics and Philosophical Description with Special Reference to Heidegger, Bultmann, Gadamer, and Wittgenstein* (Grand Rapids: Eerdmans, 1980) and *New Horizons in Hermeneutics* (Grand Rapids: Zondervan, 1992). These works offer dense and sophisticated accounts of the central figures in philosophical hermeneutics along with insights into how the philosophical issues might influence interpretation of the Bible. Many of the scholars who appear in the rest of this section became interested in theological interpretation through their own engagements with Thiselton's work.

In a similar vein, **Nicholas Wolterstorff's** *Divine Discourse: Philosophical Reflections on the Claim that God*

Speaks (Cambridge: Cambridge University Press, 1995) is the work of a philosopher examining issues of biblical interpretation. Wolterstorff's work is more narrowly focused than Thiselton's. They share a common interest in speech-act theory and a common concern to use philosphical hermeneutics to keep biblical interpretation from becoming anarchic and relativistic. Above I have noted what I take to be theological problems with this approach. Nevertheless, I do understand the concern that drives this work.

Kevin Vanhoozer has done more than anyone to bring these particular concerns to bear on theological interpretation. Beginning with *Biblical Narrative in the Philosophy of Paul Ricoeur: A Study in Hermeneutics and Theology* (Cambridge: Cambridge University Press, 1990), continuing through two large monographs, *Is There a Meaning in This Text?: The Bible, the Reader, and the Morality of Literary Knowledge* (Grand Rapids: Zondervan, 1998) and *First Theology: God, Scripture and Hermeneutics* (Downers Grove, IL: InterVarsity, 2002), and including his contributions to *Reading Scripture with the Church: Toward a Hermeneutic for Theological Interpretation* (with A. K. M. Adam, Stephen E. Fowl, and Francis Watson; Grand Rapids: Baker Academic, 2006) and his role as general editor of the *Dictionary for Theological Interpretation of the Bible* (Craig G. Bartholomew, Daniel J. Treier, and N. T. Wright, associate editors; Grand Rapids: Baker Academic, 2005), as well as his numerous essays, Vanhoozer has made a profound contribution to debates about theological interpretation. Having initially argued, using Wolterstorff among others, that theological interpretation must be regulated by the author's communicative intention, Vanhoozer has developed and modified his position over the years in ways that take much greater account of the theological problems posed to him by various critics (see his contributions to *Reading Scripture with the Church*, as well as my response in that volume). Students who would like a good introduction to Vanhoozer's earlier work from a sympathetic critic should read **D. Christopher Spinks's** monograph, *The Bible and the Crisis of Meaning: Debates on the Theological Interpretation of Scripture* (London: T. & T. Clark, 2007).

HISTORY AND HISTORICAL CRITICISM

In the chapters above, I have already indicated that it is a mistake to think of historical criticism as one thing, which one either favors or does not favor. The various critical practices that go under the name of historical criticism are not unified in terms of their object of examination; they are not necessarily compatible with each other and they are constantly under revision, negotiation, and critical self-reflection. To the extent it makes sense to use the phrase "historical criticism," it is often as a way of situating someone's disposition toward interpretive practices and attitudes typical of the guild of professional biblical scholars. That is, even if one should not think of historical criticism as a single, complex, yet identifiable thing, the phrase "historical criticism" does have a rhetorical function in debates over theological interpretation.

Although I have argued that these practices have an *ad hoc* usefulness for theological interpretation, there are those who argue that some version of these practices are necessary to interpret Scripture theologically.[2] Among these, one of

2. There may be some scholars who seriously argue that the practices of historical criticism are absolutely irrelevant for theological in-

the best examples is **Markus Bockmuehl's** *Seeing the Word: Refocusing New Testament Study* (Studies in Theological Interpretation; Grand Rapids: Baker Academic, 2006). This volume offers a very thoughtful and accessible set of arguments that indicate ways in which certain types of historical study of the New Testament can bear theological fruit. The great strength of this volume is that at its best it addresses specific historical questions and methods rather than historical criticism as a whole. **John J. Collins's** *The Bible after Babel: Historical Criticism in a Postmodern Age* (Grand Rapids: Eerdmans, 2005) is a much less successful venture. Collins does tend to use the phrase "historical criticism" as if it described one thing. His main goal in doing this seems to be to retain what he takes to be the professional integrity of biblical scholarship in the light of post-modern criticisms of various types of historiography.[3]

In a brief but fascinating volume, **Murray Rae** examines the separation of theological concerns from historical inquiry (*History and Hermeneutics*, London: T. & T. Clark, 2006). In this volume he lays out an argument for beginning to think theologically about history, or to bring historical thinking captive to Christ. This work is also characterized by concise but fair accounts of the work of a great variety of scholars. Thus, it will prove to be a valuable guide to students.[4]

---

terpretation. I think this is an untenable position and that most bashing or praising of historical criticsm is largely rhetorical.

3. See Legaspi, "What Ever Happened to Historical Criticism?"

4. Although he has not been a central figure in discussions about theological interpretation, in the numerous works of N.T. Wright one often finds arguments for the theological necessity of addressing certain historical questions.

Among those working on theological interpretation of Scripture, **A. K. M. Adam** has been a relentless and trenchant critic of the various practices of the guild of professional biblical scholars. His numerous works include *Making Sense of New Testament Theology: "Modern" Problems and Prospects* (Studies in American Biblical Hermeneutics 11; Macon, GA: Mercer University Press, 1995), *Faithful Interpretation: Reading the Bible in a Postmodern World* (Minneapolis: Fortress, 2006), two edited volumes on post-modern interpretation of the Bible (*Handbook of Postmodern Biblical Interpretation*, St. Louis: Chalice Press, 2000; and *Postmodern Interpretations of the Bible: A Reader*, St. Louis: Chalice Press, 2001), and his contributions to *Reading Scripture with the Church*. Adam's graceful prose and sharp insights provide the sort of conceptual attacks to which Collins's volume is a less than successful response.

HISTORY OF INTERPRETATION

Arguments about theological interpretation of Scripture have refocused scholarly attention on the importance of pre-modern modes of interpretation. In addition, a renewed emphasis on the ecclesial location of theological interpretation also must include a renewed appreciation for how some of the great theological interpreters of the past engaged particular texts. There are two large and ongoing projects that seek to make this history more accessible to contemporary readers. The *Ancient Christian Commentary on Scripture* (Downers Grove, IL: InterVarsity, 1998–) offers for each verse of a biblical book a chain of brief citations from interpreters from the post–New Testament period down to 750 CE. As a reference tool, these volumes are best used to direct students to the sources which can then be studied in greater detail and in a wider context. *The Church's Bible* (Grand Rapids: Eerdmans, 2003–) includes longer passages from various patristic and medieval interpreters. Some of these had heretofore not been available in English.

In addition to these reference works, **R. R. Reno** and **John O'Keefe** have written a very fine introduction to early Christian biblical interpretation entitled *Sanctified Vision: An Introduction to Early Christian Interpretation of the Bible* (Grand Rapids: Brazos, 2005). Further, **Jason Byasee's** volume, *Praise Seeking Understanding: Reading the Psalms with Augustine* (Radical Traditions; Grand Rapids: Eerdmans, 2007), is another useful monograph here. Both of these works go beyond simply analyzing the reading strategies of patristic interpreters in order to show *why* they read and *how* their reading of Scripture might influence our own. In this regard **Lewis Ayres's** *Nicea and Its Legacy: An Approach to Fourth-Century Trinitarian Theology* (Oxford: Oxford University Press, 2004) is also instructive. Although not directly about theological interpretation, Ayres explores both the ways in which pro-Nicene theology was profoundly scriptural and the theological culture that sustained pro-Nicene interpretive practices. In this regard, students of theological interpretation may find the final chapter of the book most helpful.

Theological Approaches to the Old Testament

It would be hard to overestimate the influence of the work of the late Brevard Childs. From his early work, *Biblical Theology in Crisis* (Philadelphia: Westminster, 1970) and his commentary, *The Book of Exodus: A Critical, Theological Commentary* (The Old Testament Library; Philadelphia: Westminster, 1974), through his seminal *Introduction to the Old Testament as Scripture* (Philadelphia: Fortress, 1979) and his *Biblical Theology of the Old and New Testaments: Theological Reflection on the Christian Bible* (Minneapolis: Fortress, 1993), Childs set a forth a rigorous and well-thought-out program for interpreting Scripture theologically. For many of those engaged in the current debates, Childs was the person who was able to show the importance and possibilities of reading Scripture theologically in a guild of scholars that seemed strongly committed to keeping theology at arm's length. In many respects, Childs's work is ably carried forward by **Christopher Seitz**. His most significant contributions to debates over theological interpretation include *Word without End: The Old Testament as Abiding Theological Witness* (Grand Rapids: Eerdmans, 1998), *Figured Out: Typology and Providence in Christian Scripture* (Louisville, KY: Westminster John Knox, 2001), and *Prophecy and Hermeneutics: A New Introduction to the Prophets* (Grand Rapids: Baker, 2007). Both Childs and Seitz are appropriately diligent in reminding theological interpreters of the abiding significance of the Old Testament. Even those who do not follow their larger theological and theoretical proposals cannot downplay the significance of their diligent reminders.

Few scholars are able to combine a graceful writing style, a keen analytical mind, and a charitable disposition toward the work of others as well as **R. W. L. Moberly**. His works include *The Old Testament of the Old Testament: Patriarchal Narratives and Mosaic Yahwism* (Overtures to Biblical Theology; Minneapolis: Fortress, 1992), *From Eden* *to Golgotha: Essays in Biblical Theology* (Atlanta: Scholars Press, 1992), and *The Bible, Theology, and Faith: A Study of Abraham and Jesus* (Cambridge Studies in Christian Doctrine; Cambridge: Cambridge University Press, 2000). Although influenced by Childs, he would not be called a follower of Childs's "canonical approach." His work is characterized by close attention to biblical texts and the creative injection of theological insight into the reading of those texts.

ROMAN CATHOLIC CONTRIBUTIONS

When one looks at most of the major institutional organs that arise from and support the current interest in theological interpretation of Scripture, one finds very few Roman Catholic contributors. See for example:

> *Ex Auditu: An International Journal of the Theological Interpretation of Scripture.* Eugene, OR: Pickwick, 1985–.
>
> *Journal of Theological Interpretation.* Winona Lake, IN: Eisenbrauns, 2007–.
>
> The Two Horizons New Testament Commentary. Grand Rapids: Eerdmans, 2007–.
>
> Brazos Theological Commentary on the Bible. Grand Rapids: Brazos, 2006–.
>
> Studies in Theological Interpretation. Grand Rapids: Baker Academic, 2006–.
>
> Vanhoozer, Kevin, editor. *Dictionary for the Theological Interpretation of the Bible*. Grand Rapids: Baker Academic, 2005.

The one area that might be an exception here concerns work on the history of interpretation. This in part reflects the Roman Catholic Church's ambivalent relationship to modern biblical criticism from the encyclical *Providentissimus Deus* (1893) down to the present. While that ambivalence never entirely disappears, *Divino Afflante Spiritu* (1943) initiated the full-blooded entrance of Roman Catholic scholars into the guild of professional biblical scholars. The sharp separation between biblical studies and theology that developed in Protestant scholarship over a long period of time took place at a fast pace in Roman Catholicism, so much so that by the end of the 20th century it was unclear what made Catholic biblical scholarship Catholic.

In terms of theological interpretation, one can situate Catholic scholars by their response to the document *Interpretation of the Bible in the Church*, issued by the Pontifical Biblical Commission in 1993.[5] Scholars such as **Luke Timothy Johnson** (*The Creed: What Christians Believe and Why It Matters* [New York: Doubleday, 2003]; *The Real Jesus: The Misguided Quest for the Historical Jesus and the Truth of the Traditional Gospels* [San Francisco: HarperSanFrancisco, 1996]; and *Living Jesus: Learning the Heart of the Gospel* [San Francisco: HarperSanFrancisco, 1999]), **Sandra Schneiders** (*The Revelatory Text: Interpreting the New Testament as Sacred Scripture* [2nd ed.; Collegeville, MN: Liturgical, 1999]), **Gary Anderson** (*The Genesis of Perfection: Adam and Eve in Jewish and Christian Imagination* [Louisville: Westminster John Knox, 2001]), and **Matthew Levering** (*Scripture and Metaphysics: Aquinas and the Renewal of Trinitarian*

5. See Murphy, "What Is Catholic about Catholic Biblical Scholarship?"; Johnson, "So What's Catholic about It?"; and Ayres and Fowl, "(Mis)Reading the Face of God."

Theology [Challenges in Contemporary Theology; Malden, MA: Blackwell, 2004] and *Participatory Biblical Exegesis: A Theology of Biblical Interpretation* [Reading the Scriptures; Notre Dame, IN: University of Notre Dame Press, 2008]) represent a movement among Catholic scholars that question the dominance of historical-critical modes of interpretation and seek to bring their Catholicism to bear on biblical interpretation. Along these lines, one might also consider the newly launched commentary series, The Catholic Commentary on Sacred Scripture (Grand Rapids: Baker Academic, 2008–).

Other Interesting and Interested Parties

In the lists above, I have tried to replicate the topics and emphases related in this companion. As one might expect, there are scholars whose work does not easily fit into these predetermined categories. Their writing, however, is worthy of attention, and I will use this section to speak about these works in alphabetical order.

Ellen Davis and **Richard Hays** are both first-rate readers of Scripture in their own right. They collaborated to edit a volume entitled *The Art of Reading Scripture* (Grand Rapids: Eerdmans, 2003), which contains a rich variety of essays from theologians and biblical scholars addressing issues of specific relevance to theological interpretation, including selected sermons.

Over the past decade **Michael Gorman** has written a variety of books and articles that touch on central issues of theological interpretation. Beginning students would benefit enormously from his edited volume, *Scripture: An Ecumenical Introduction to the Bible and its Interpretation* (Peabody, MA: Hendrickson, 2005). In addition, his monograph,

Cruciformity: Paul's Narrative Spirituality of the Cross (Grand Rapids: Eerdmans, 2001), and two subsequent books on the same theme (*Apostle of the Crucified Lord: A Theological Introduction to Paul and His Letters* [Grand Rapids: Eerdmans, 2004] and *Inhabiting the Cruciform God: Kenosis, Justification, and Theosis in Paul's Narrative Soteriology* [Grand Rapids: Eerdmans, 2009]) are excellent examples of interpreting Paul's epistles theologically.

There are few professional theologians who really take the time to work their way into both biblical texts and the treatment of those texts by professional biblical scholars. When this happens, however, the result is almost always theologically very interesting and extremely important for the practice of theological interpretation. One of the best examples of this is **Douglas Harink's** *Paul among the Postliberals: Pauline Theology beyond Christendom and Modernity* (Grand Rapids: Brazos, 2003).

I have already mentioned **Daniel Treier's** *Introducing Theological Interpretation of Scripture: Recovering a Christian Practice* (Grand Rapids: Baker Academic, 2008) in the introduction to this companion. There I tried to explain what I take to be some of the differences between an introduction to theological interpretation and this companion. Let me simply reiterate here that Treier's is a fine book and well worth the attention one devotes to it.

For a number of years **Robert Wall** has written extensively on two themes directly related to theological interpretation. First, Wall is interested in the canonical shaping of the New Testament particularly with regard to the relationships between Acts and the various letters of the New Testament. The volume he wrote with Eugene Lemcio, *The New Testament* *as Canon: A Reader in Canonical Criticism* (Sheffield: JSOT Press, 1992) is a good place to begin reading in this area. As an extension of this interest, Wall has been probing issues around the Rule of Faith and theological interpretation, especially in the light of particular confessional considerations (see "Reading the Bible from within Our Traditions: The 'Rule of Faith' in Theological Hermeneutics," in *Between Two Horizons: Spanning New Testament Studies and Systematic Theology*, edited by Joel B. Green and Max Turner, 88–108; Grand Rapids: Eerdmans, 2000).

One of the most prolific, yet hardest to classify, scholars writing on theological interpretation is **Francis Watson**. The most relevant of his works include *Text, Church, and World: Biblical Interpretation in Theological Perspective* (Grand Rapids: Eerdmans, 1994) and *Text and Truth: Redefining Biblical Theology* (Grand Rapids: Eerdmans, 1997), as well as his contribution to *Reading Scripture with the Church*. Watson is an astute critic of biblical scholarship and its presumptions against theological concerns. As a general rule, I find that his constructive proposals are governed more by the concerns of professional theologians rather than the life and practice of the church.

John Webster is a theologian who has always had a strong interest in Scripture and its interpretation. His small volume *Holy Scripture: A Dogmatic Sketch* (Current Issues in Theology; Cambridge: Cambridge University Press, 2003) is a wonderfully thoughtful attempt to overcome modern theology's separation of a doctrine of revelation from its properly dependent relationship to the Christian doctrine of God. In this light, one can also mention **Telford Work's** volume, *Living and Active: Scripture in the Economy of Salvation* (Grand Rapids: Eerdmans, 2002).

Works Cited

Adam, A. K. M. *Making Sense of New Testament Theology: "Modern" Problems and Prospects.* Studies in American Biblical Hermeneutics 11. Macon, GA: Mercer University Press, 1995.

———. "Docetism, Käsemann, and Christology: Why Historical Criticism Can't Protect Christological Orthodoxy." *Scottish Journal of Theology* 49 (1996) 391–410.

Augustine. *On Christian Teaching.* Translated with an introduction and notes by R. P. H. Green. World's Classics. New York: Oxford University Press, 1997.

Austin, J. L. *How to Do Things with Words.* The William James Lectures, 1955. Cambridge, MA: Harvard University Press, 1962.

Ayres, Lewis, and Stephen E. Fowl. "(Mis)Reading the Face of God: The Interpretation of the Bible in the Church." *Theological Studies* 60 (1999) 513–28.

Barr, James. *The Concept of Biblical Theology: An Old Testament Perspective.* Minneapolis: Fortress, 1999.

Barth, Karl. *The Doctrine of the Word of God. Church Dogmatics I, Part 2.* Translated by G. W. Bromiley, edited by T. F. Torrance. Edinburgh: T. & T. Clark, 1956.

Blowers, Paul M. "The *Regula Fidei* and the Narrative Character of Early Christian Faith." *Pro Ecclesia* 6 (1997) 199–228.

Brazos Theological Commentary on the Bible. Grand Rapids: Brazos, 2006–.

Brett, Mark G. *Biblical Criticism in Crisis?: The Impact of the Canonical Approach on Old Testament Studies.* Cambridge: Cambridge University Press, 1991.

———. "Motives and Intentions in Genesis 1." *Journal of Theological Studies* 42 (1991) 1–16.

Caird, G. B. *New Testament Theology*. Completed and edited by L. D. Hurst. Oxford: Oxford University Press, 1994.

Childs, Brevard. "Toward Recovering Theological Exegesis." *Pro Ecclesia* 6 (1997) 16–26.

Davis, Ellen F., and Richard B. Hays, editors. *The Art of Reading Scripture*. Grand Rapids: Eerdmans, 2003.

Fowl, Stephen E. *Engaging Scripture: A Model for Theological Interpretation*. Challenges in Contemporary Theology. Malden, MA: Blackwell, 1998.

———. *Philippians*. The Two Horizons New Testament Commentary. Grand Rapids: Eerdmans, 2005.

———. "Theological and Ideological Strategies of Biblical Interpretation." In *Scripture: An Ecumenical Introduction to the Bible and Its Interpretation*, edited by Michael J. Gorman, 163–76. Peabody, MA: Hendrickson, 2005.

Fowl, Stephen E., and L. Gregory Jones. *Reading in Communion: Scripture and Ethics in Christian Life*. Grand Rapids: Eerdmans, 1991. Reprinted, Eugene, OR: Wipf & Stock, 1998.

Frei, Hans W. *The Eclipse of Biblical Narrative: A Study in Eighteenth and Nineteenth Century Hermeneutics*. New Haven, CT: Yale University Press, 1974.

Greer, Rowan A. "The Christian Bible and Its Interpretation." In *Early Biblical Interpretation*, by James L. Kugel and Rowan A. Greer, 107–208. Library of Early Christianity 3. Philadelphia: Westminster, 1986.

Johnson, Luke Timothy. "So What's Catholic about It? The State of Catholic Biblical Scholarship." *Commonweal*, January 16, 1998, 12–16.

Journal of Theological Interpretation. Winona Lake, IN: Eisenbrauns, 2007–.

Käsemann, Ernst. "Vom theologischen Recht historisch-kritischer Exegese." *Zeitschrift für Theologie und Kirche* 64 (1967) 259–81.

Legaspi, Michael C. "What Ever Happened to Historical Criticism?" *Journal of Religion and Society* 9 (2007) 1–11.

Murphy, Roland E. "What Is Catholic about Catholic Biblical Scholarship?—Revisited." *Biblical Theology Bulletin* 28 (1998) 112–19.

O'Keefe, John J., and Russell R. Reno. *Sanctified Vision: An Introduction to Early Christian Interpretation of the Bible*. Baltimore: Johns Hopkins University Press, 2005.

Ollenberger, Ben C. "Biblical Theology: Situating the Discipline." In *Understanding the Word: Essays in Honor of Bernard W. Anderson*, edited by James T. Butler, Edgar W. Conrad, and Ben C. Ollenberger, 37–62. Journal for the Study of the Old Testament Supplement Series 37. Sheffield: JSOT Press, 1985.

Origen. *On First Principles.* Translated with an introduction and notes by G. W. Butterworth. 1936. Reprint, Gloucester, MA: Peter Smith, 1973.

Pontifical Biblical Commission. *Interpretation of the Bible in the Church.* Washington, DC: United States Catholic Conference, 1993.

Radner, Ephraim. *The End of the Church: A Pneumatology of Christian Division in the West.* Grand Rapids: Eerdmans, 1998.

Ratzinger, Jospeh Cardinal (Pope Benedict XVI). *Church, Ecumenism, and Politics: New Essays in Ecclesiology.* New York: Crossroad, 1988.

Robinson, Anthony B., and Robert W. Wall. *Called to Be Church: The Book of Acts for a New Day.* Grand Rapids: Eerdmans, 2006.

Rowe, C. Kavin. "New Testament Theologies: The Revival of a Discipline: A Review of Recent Contributions to the Field." *Journal of Biblical Literature* 125 (2006) 393–419.

Schlatter, Adolf. "The Theology of the New Testament and Dogmatics." In *The Nature of New Testament Theology: The Contribution of William Wrede and Adolf Schlatter*, edited, translated, and with an introduction by Robert Morgan, 117–66. Studies in Biblical Theology 25. London: SCM, 1973.

Searle, John R. *Speech Acts: An Essay in the Philosophy of Language.* London: Cambridge University Press, 1969.

Skinner, Quentin. "Motives, Intentions and the Interpretation of Texts." *New Literary History* 3 (1972) 393–408.

Strawn, Brent. "Docetism, Käsemann and Christology: Can Historical Criticism Help Christological Orthodoxy (and Other Theology) After All?" *Journal of Theological Interpretation* 2:2 (2008) 161–80.

Tanner, Norman P., editor. *Decrees of the Ecumenical Councils.* 2 vols. Washington, DC: Georgetown University Press, 1990.

Treier, Daniel J. *Introducing Theological Interpretation of Scripture: Recovering a Christian Practice.* Grand Rapids: Baker Academic, 2008.

The Two Horizons New Testament Commentary. Grand Rapids: Eerdmans, 2007–.

Vanhoozer, Kevin J. *Is There a Meaning in This Text?: The Bible, The Reader and the Morality of Literary Knowledge.* Grand Rapids: Zondervan, 1998.

———, editor. *Dictionary for the Theological Interpretation of the Bible.* Grand Rapids: Baker Academic, 2005.

Wall, Robert. "Reading the Bible from within Our Traditions: The 'Rule of Faith' in Theological Hermeneutics." In *Between Two Horizons: Spanning New Testament Studies and Systematic Theology,* edited by Joel B. Green and Max Turner, 88–108. Grand Rapids: Eerdmans, 2000.

———. "Facilitating Scripture's Future Role among Wesleyans." In *Reading the Bible in Wesleyan Ways: Some Constructive Proposals,* edited by Barry L. Callen and Richard P. Thompson, 107–22. Kansas City: Beacon Hill, 2004.

Webster, John. *Holy Scripture: A Dogmatic Sketch.* Current Issues in Theology. Cambridge: Cambridge University Press, 2003.

Work, Telford. *Living and Active: Scripture in the Economy of Salvation.* Sacra Doctrina. Grand Rapids: Eerdmans, 2002.

Wright, Christopher J. H. *The Mission of God: Unlocking the Bible's Grand Narrative.* Downers Grove, IL: IVP Academic, 2006.

Made in the USA
San Bernardino, CA
11 November 2015